UNLICENSED MEDICINE

RELEASING ANCESTRAL TRAUMA AND UNLEASHING THE POWER OF YOUR LINEAGE

by

Dr. Meher Chahal

Unlicensed Medicine: Releasing Ancestral Trauma and Unleashing the Power of Your Lineage
Written by Dr. Meher Chahal

This book is a work of nonfiction. It represents the accuracy of the events mentioned to the best of the author's recollection. Some names in the book have been replaced to maintain the privacy of certain individuals.

The information contained in this book is provided for educational purposes only and should not be construed as medical, legal, or financial advice. Readers are strongly encouraged to consult with a qualified and licensed professional who can provide advice tailored to their individual circumstances. Laws, regulations, and financial practices vary across countries, states, and regions. Market conditions, returns, and outcomes will differ over time and cannot be guaranteed. While every effort has been made to provide accurate and timely information at the time of writing, we make no representations or warranties regarding completeness, accuracy, or applicability. We are not making any official legal or financial recommendations. The examples, figures, and principles presented herein are for illustrative and educational purposes only. Any decisions you make are solely your responsibility.

Paperback ISBN: 978-1-967587-34-6
eBook ISBN: 978-1-967587-35-3

It is an absolute honor to dedicate this book as a tribute to my ancestors. I truly believe that our soul chooses our parents and lineage for a higher purpose.

I would also love to dedicate this book to any reader/listener who has struggled or felt alone in their healing journey. I hope this book makes you feel deeply seen and understood.

TABLE OF CONTENTS

Warning: This Book May Cause Sudden Self-Awareness.

Side effects include recognizing unhealthy family patterns, getting sick of your own shit, an uncontrollable urge to heal, and audacious authenticity. Proceed with caution.

Introduction

The privilege of a lifetime is to become who you truly are.
—Carl Jung

I still remember the look in Meera's eyes—the sheer terror—when I told her about my family history. I sat in her cozy Park Slope apartment, describing my mother's schizophrenia, the murder in my lineage, the addiction, sexual abuse, and repeating patterns. She took notes as I narrated the events of my lineage and looked at me with concerned, widened eyes but didn't say much. It was one of the first times in my life that I felt profoundly seen, heard, and understood on a deep level.

Fuck, I thought as I heard myself say everything out loud, *I actually have a lot of family trauma.* The truth was, before that moment, I didn't think I had any trauma. After all, I grew up rich and privileged. My childhood wasn't that bad. I was getting by just fine. I was a *doctor* after all. I had a respectable job. So what was I complaining about?

And yet, I was there in the apartment of a woman I'd found on Google, whose quiet, sage-like inner confidence and safe energy drew me to tell her every dark detail about my past.

"Oh yeah, there was a murder. And yeah, my mother has schizophrenia. And yeah, I basically grew up alone. And yeah, I had, like, all forms of abuse." The entire time I kept my composure. I didn't think it was a problem. To me, it was just life. Like there was nothing extraordinary about what I was saying. I thought, *Doesn't everybody experience this?*

You know that internet meme where there's a dog sitting at a table inside a house engulfed in flames and the speech bubble above his head says, "This is fine." Yeah, that was my life. I was utterly oblivious to the emotional pain that had been trapped inside me for so long. I had been living life from the neck up, stuck in my head and completely disconnected from my body and real feelings. I often didn't realize how much trauma I was holding.

We don't see the shadows we live in. They are so deeply woven into our family stories that they feel normal. I didn't realize how much I was carrying until someone else saw it in me—the rage, the grief, the unprocessed trauma of generations past— all silently shaping my life. It wasn't until I sat in a stranger's apartment, watching the shock on her face, that I started to question: *What have I inherited? Am I doomed for life? And how much of this is actually mine to carry forward?*

GENERATIONAL PATTERNS

The patterns we inherit don't introduce themselves. They don't knock politely on the door and ask to come into your life. Absolutely not. They sneak in through your DNA like they own the place. They live in us quietly, shaping our choices, fate, our relationships, and our sense of self before we ever realize they're there.

These patterns are our ancestral shadows. They're unconscious manifestations of trauma, grief, addiction, and survival mechanisms. And they don't begin with us. They're passed down through our family line often in ways we can't see. Some of them are obvious, like addiction running through generations, but others are more insidious, masquerading as personality traits, self-sabotage, or inability to break free from old cycles.

These shadows are mostly unconscious. They come from a childlike innocence, a basic need for the child to belong to their family and their ancestry. We carry these unconsciously out of loyalty and childlike love so we can continue to belong to our tribe.

From the moment we are born, our survival depends on our connection to our family. A child will do anything—anything—to maintain that bond, even if it means sacrificing their own truth, or worse, life. It is pure innocent love. If our family carries shame, we inherit it through conditioning and epigenetics. If they never process their grief, we carry it in our nervous systems. If they have been stuck in cycles of trauma for generations, we will unconsciously repeat those same patterns, because to do anything else feels like betrayal. I mean I don't know about you, but it's certainly not fun being the odd one out of your family.

In Family Constellations (FC) therapy, staying loyal to our family gives us a "good" conscience, while betraying that loyalty, by living differently and accepting the guilt that comes with it, gives us a "bad" conscience but also freedom. This is why so many of us stay stuck and self-sabotage. It's why we live lives that don't feel fully ours. It's not because we're lazy, incapable, or stupid; it's because on some unconscious level, we are loyal to our lineage. We follow the unspoken fate and rules of our ancestors, even when they no longer serve us. *After all, who am I to live a full life, when my ancestors couldn't?*

Ancestral shadows don't always look like trauma. Sometimes they show up in unexpected ways such as addictions, mental illnesses, toxic family dynamics, physical illnesses, and the list goes on. For example, women make up four out of five individuals with an autoimmune illness diagnosis.[1] Is it a coincidence that the feminine has been repressed for centuries? That only a few hundred years ago, women who spoke out were hunted as witches and hung or burned for the crime of holding wisdom and independence? For speaking their truth and using their voices?

Sigmund Freud said depression is anger turned inwards. Women's voices, their anger, their pain have been silenced. An angry woman? Oh, you're not feminine or soft enough. Shame on you. But the thing is, as much as we push the anger down or try to ignore it, it doesn't evaporate into thin air. Unprocessed anger can fuel stress responses that may worsen health, including thyroid disease and neurological illness such as multiple sclerosis.

---

1 National Institutes of Health, "Understanding Sex Differences in Autoimmune Disease," *NIH Research Matters*, December 12, 2023, https://www.nih.gov/news-events/nih-research-matters/understanding-sex-differences-autoimmune-disease.

You may have heard before that emotion is energy in motion. And repressed emotion is trapped energy. It means that no matter how hard we try, we can't make our trauma disappear into thin air. This is why talk therapy keeps us stuck in intellectualisation. But what we can do is transmute that stuck energy into something powerful so the energy can finally flow freely. In Jungian alchemy, an inner transformation that's called "turning lead into gold." It's the process of reforming our heaviest, darkest experiences into wisdom, growth, and personal power. And essentially, that's what this book is about.

In my own family, this stuck energy created patterns that repeated with eerie precision. My great-grandmother committed a murder. Two generations later, my mother developed schizophrenia. And the kicker is, my family's story isn't unique. One of the most shocking things Meera told me as I sat in her living room in Brooklyn was that she'd heard my story before and more than once. My family's story was part of a pattern she'd seen, where one of the progeny of families who had experienced murders behind closed doors ended up developing schizophrenia.

It might sound "woo-woo" or like superstition or some sort of cosmic curse making this happen, but it's not. There's actually a scientific explanation for it called epigenetics. In a nut shell, epigenetics is the science of how our environment, experiences, and trauma can switch certain genes on or off, including parts of our DNA. This was once dismissed by scientists as "junk DNA" because they didn't appear to code for proteins or have a known function. We now know these sections can play a role in regulating which genes are expressed.[2] We can inherit more than hair color or eye shape; we can also inherit patterns of pain. In fact, when your grandmother was pregnant with your mother, you were already the egg inside your mom's ovaries, so any stressors your grandmother experienced were, in a sense, firsthand trauma for you too because you existed as a cell within her body.[3]

YOUR FAMILY'S ANCESTRAL SHADOWS

Maybe your story isn't as dramatic as mine. But it's still true: All secrets make you sick. So sick. Your skeleton closet may not hide a murder, but there are still shadows there. Maybe you carry the unspoken grief of a grandmother who never got to make her own choices in life. Perhaps you bear the resentment of a lineage of women told to shrink themselves, to be less than they were because shame keeps you obedient and tied to your tribe. Or maybe you've inherited the fear of scarcity from generations who had to survive on less, even though that's no longer your reality. Or worse, you might be unconsciously identifying with the fate of a deceased ancestor who was aborted or ostracized.

Our ancestors deserve to be honored, revered, and remembered. It's because of their sacrifices that we are alive today. But we also need to unburden ourselves of the fates that aren't ours to carry and return them with love and respect.

---

2 Ko YA, Susztak K. Epigenomics: the science of no-longer-junk DNA. Why study it in chronic kidney disease? Semin Nephrol. 2013 Jul;33(4):354-62. doi: 10.1016/j.semnephrol.2013.05.007. PMID: 24011577; PMCID: PMC3815533.

3 F. Serpeloni, et al., "Grandmaternal stress during pregnancy and DNA methylation of the third generation: an epigenome-wide association study," (2017).

When we do this intentionally, we can begin to choose healthier ways of belonging, rather than repeating the same unhealthy patterns or dynamics. Setting boundaries or having no contact doesn't end the story.

In Family Constellations therapy, *the field* (also called the knowing field, the systemic field, or the family soul/unconscious)[4] refers to an energetic, transgenerational system that holds information, emotions, unconscious loyalties, and entanglements influencing family members across generations.[5] It's considered a collective energy or morphic field that participants tap into during constellation sessions. The practitioner channels this energy, allowing the healing that needs to unfold to do so in its own way.[6] It's the language of the soul not the conscious mind.

There's no real escaping this. The field, that deep ancestral web of belonging, will always pull you back toward equilibrium.

Shadows don't just vanish. They will keep manifesting in your family. Patterns and hidden loyalties don't disappear or burn to ash with the cremation or burial of your ancestors' body. At some point, one person in the family must wake up. One person must see the dysfunction and think, *This isn't right. This isn't how I want to live.* The pain becomes too much to bear. That person is often labeled the black sheep. They're the one

---

4 *Hellinger Institute / Family Constellation Ireland*, "What Is Family Constellations?" accessed August 13, 2025, https://familyconstellation.ie.

5 Center for Applied Cultural Studies (CAS-E), "Family Constellation Therapy in the Context of Esotericism," last modified November 22, 2023, https://cas-e.de/2023/11/22/family-constellation-therapy-in-the-context-of-esotericism/.

6 Rupert Sheldrake, "Morphic Fields and Family Constellations," YouTube video, Feb 17, 2020, https://www.youtube.com/watch?v=ty5lz9mVezU.

who doesn't fit in, who questions the rules, and who chooses a different path.

Some people think that the black sheep is saying, with a sense of entitlement, "Yay! I'm the cycle-breaker! Look at me, doing life differently! Fuck you all, I'm so much better than you!" But that's not what it's actually like. The price of freedom is loneliness. The path of individuation is painful. You have to be able to handle the guilt of betraying your family, the shame of choosing yourself, and the fear of not belonging and being unloved.

Being the black sheep isn't living out a rebellion. It's about responsibility. It means carrying the weight of generations of unprocessed trauma and choosing to bring it into light instead of passing it down. It means making the unconscious conscious, no matter how painful. The writer Joseph Campbell said one of my favorite lines about this: "If the path before you is clear you're probably on someone else's." Being the black sheep means forging your own path, and that my friend, takes courage.

We do have a choice. No matter what cards fate dealt us in our childhoods, we still have freewill. We cannot control our parents, siblings, boyfriend, girlfriend, or anyone else's fate, but I chose to believe that we can transform our own.

Choosing to heal is the easy part. The actual healing part? That's hard AF. When you start questioning the patterns you've inherited, your whole life feels as if it's unraveling. You realize you're carrying things that aren't yours, and you start asking:

If I'm not who my family expects me to be...then who the hell am I? That's the billion dollar question.

THE HARD WORK

I am Punjabi. I love being Punjabi. I have deep reverence for my lineage. My ancestors are a people known for their boldness, courage, and unwavering strength. They're WARRIORS. But like everything in life, strength has a shadow side. In my family, it manifested as defensiveness and entitlement caused by generations of unprocessed trauma. We often carry pain the way we carry pride, which is fiercely, silently, and without question. In Punjabi culture, trauma isn't something you address. You numb it with alcohol, you power through, and you keep going. "Just be resilient" becomes your daily mantra. We have forgotten that we are no longer on a physical battlefield and it's now safe to put down the sword.

So I learned to power through. I kept going. I was sprinting to gather all the external validation and scholarly badges of accomplishments I was expected to achieve. I became a doctor. I was specialising in psychiatry. Isn't that hilarious? Mom's schizophrenic, and her kid grows up to be a psychiatrist. Classic wounded healer archetype. Couldn't save Mom from her fate, so I tried to save everyone else from theirs. Looking back now, I can see it so clearly. At the time I was in total denial about my *mother wound*, the emotional pain and sense of lack that comes from a mother's unavailability, neglect, or inability to nurture. It's actually pretty funny to see how convinced I was that I was totally unaffected by her apathy, distance, and sickness.

Choosing psychiatry felt like control. It felt like answers. I thought that if I could understand mental illness and if I could help other people, maybe I could save others from their fate.

And then I saw how psychiatry actually worked. I saw how my mom had been in and out of treatment for decades, and how little had actually changed. I finally understood the cocktail of all the different antipsychotics she was given, how doctors tried medication after medication on her like a guinea pig. When I became a psychiatry resident physician, my integrity was challenged. I had to admit people to the psych ward, diagnose, medicate, physically restrain them, and then finally send them on their way, without ever actually healing anything.

That's when I started to realize: Psychiatry doesn't have all the answers. It isn't even asking all the right questions.

I saw people who cycled in and out of psychiatric care without any real transformation like a damn revolving door. And most of all, I started to see it in my own life, how even with all my medical training, I had stayed completely blind to my own trauma. The world tells us that if we have degrees, credentials, and clinical language, we're somehow immune to trauma, we're elevated above the pain of our "helpless" patients. But trauma doesn't care about titles. I was living proof of that.

When I told my dad in 11th grade I was considering some other career besides being a doctor, he didn't talk to me for three days. And logically, his anger made sense. Who walks away from a stable, respected medical career? So as an obedient, loving, eldest daughter of an Indian family, and of course choosing safety over the unknown, I gave in.

I left residency two weeks before my third year of training. It was during this time that I found Family Constellations. Or to be more accurate, I finally gave in to the infinite synchronicities that had been pulling me toward Family Constellations for some time.

For a while, every time I would open up to someone about my family's history, whether it was a Reiki master or a spiritual coach, they would widen their eyes and ask me, "Have you heard of Family Constellations?" I learned it was a type of group therapy that helps people identify and address issues in their inherited family relationships.

But you don't start therapy when things are manageable. You start when you are on your knees. When life cracks you open so violently that you have no choice but to confront what you've been avoiding.

For me it happened when my dog went into heart failure. I truly believe Goofy came into my life to teach me unconditional love, to show me how to live from the heart. He was my first stable, secure attachment and when he got sick it destroyed me. Bringing him to the ICU pulled me into my *dark night of the soul.*

It was while I was on my knees in the ICU, waiting to hear from the doctor, that I pulled out my phone and googled Family Constellations. I found this Indian woman and immediately resonated with what she was saying. It was not only because of our shared cultural background, but because she understood, firsthand, what it meant to be an Indian woman choosing her own path. Not defying exactly but the courage to individuate and to break away from familial expectations, and, in many ways, to not belong.

Her parents were Indian doctors, and she had taken a radically different path. She was a single mother who went from living on food stamps to earning six figures within a year, only to be disowned by her family for following her truth. What a woman!

WHO IS THIS BOOK FOR?

Breaking the cycle isn't easy. It's lonely, disorienting, and forces you to confront the very patterns that once made you feel safe. When you start this work, everything you thought you knew about yourself begins to unravel. You start to see the ways you've been unconsciously repeating your family's story, playing out dynamics that were set in motion long before you were born. And once you see it, you can't unsee it.

One of the most important things I hope this book offers is a deeper loving awareness of our shadows. How do you identify your shadows? The parts of yourself you shame, deny, and repress? Where do they live in your body? How do they shape our reactions and how can we integrate them rather than unconsciously acting them out?

But here's the thing—awareness is not enough. Just knowing that you carry ancestral shadows won't break the pattern. I hate to tell you this, but understanding your trauma won't heal it. You can't just acknowledge your past, light some sage, pull some Tarot cards, chant a few Om Shantis, and suddenly all your trauma is gone. If healing were that simple, I'd have a gold medal in the trauma Olympics for intellectualizing my pain.

However, this is hope. I feel somehow hope saves lives. And if hope is what you've been looking for, this book is for you. Hope saved my life multiple times when I was struggling with my mental health in my 20s.

Healing takes work. Deep, uncomfortable *shadow work*. It's standing in the mirror and seeing the parts of yourself you've spent your whole life avoiding. It's realizing that the things you judge in others are actually the things you haven't accepted in yourself. As Carl Jung said, "Everything that irritates us about others, can lead us to an understanding of ourselves."

It takes radical responsibility. It takes the ability to know that even though these patterns didn't start with you, you are the one responsible to heal them. And it takes the ability to tolerate guilt and to tolerate the shame that comes with being the one brave enough to be different. And it takes strength to tolerate the judgments close ones will put you through when they are triggered by your growth.

Too often, healing focuses only on childhood wounds. Your mother did this, so now you struggle with that. Your father punished you for this, so now you don't express yourself. And while those things might be true, they are not the whole story.

The work with Family Constellations stretches our lenses ever wider. Some of the traumas we carry have nothing to do with our personal experiences. They are inherited and passed down unprocessed through generations.

I experienced this firsthand in a Family Constellation workshop when I suddenly felt a wave of murderous rage. It wasn't just anger. It wasn't just irritation. It was a primal, bodily urge to kill. My hand literally tingled, burned to strike, to destroy. It was terrifying.

A year earlier, I wouldn't have even admitted to having thoughts like this. I would have buried them under shame. Or worse case scenario I would have found myself locked up in the psych ward for expressing suicidal or homicidal ideations. But in that workshop, I was able to bring these feelings to light without judgment. My facilitator, also trained in somatic experiencing, held space for me as I processed the emotion through my body.

Still, I couldn't understand it. Why was I feeling this way? Yes, my grandmother had a terrible temper, but this experience went beyond that. It went all the way back to my great-grandmother. From the ancestral shadows that kindled the anger within her rage and the trauma that continued to be passed down her lineage without someone to break the cycle, she carried a burden too heavy to bear. The rage I was feeling was part of a larger ancestral story, one that hadn't started with me but had lived in my family's lineage, unprocessed, for generations. Anger often arises when our personal boundaries have been violated again and again. In my lineage, those violations had deep roots: My great-great-grandmother was the only heir to a large sum of land, yet she was locked away in a mental hospital and spent the prime of her life there. Her voice was silenced, her boundaries ignored; and that violation echoed down the line, teaching every woman who came after her that silence was safer than rage.

WHAT YOU CAN EXPECT FROM THIS BOOK

I left Western medicine to follow my soul's calling, to step into my life's true purpose. As the title of this book states: I am not licensed to practice in the United States. And you know what? I'm glad I'm not. If I were, I probably never would have written this book. Not having that license, that box to fit in, has given me the freedom to speak my truth freely, unfiltered, and unapologetically.

My medicine isn't the kind you can measure in milligrams or prescribe in neat little bottles. It's the medicine of the body, the soul, and the lineage. It's somatic work, shadow work, Family Constellations, and the ancestral wisdom passed down through generations who were never "licensed" by any institution and yet knew how to work with rhythm, ritual, plants, and spirit.

I walked away from the title of "doctor" because the system was failing what I knew to be true; real healing often happens outside the sterile walls of a clinic. My own healing didn't come from protocols or prescriptions. It came from listening to my body, honoring my ancestors, and reclaiming the parts of me that Western medicine had no language for. That is the heart of *Unlicensed Medicine*.

I believe Systemic and Family Constellations are transformational. This is one of the missing keys to the puzzle of a healing journey. These processes help us connect the dots beyond our own lifetime. Instead of looking at trauma only through the lens of personal experience, we begin to see how these patterns of unfortunate tragedies our ancestors endured, and unconsciously repeated, were passed down, until someone, somewhere, decides to wake up and break the cycle.

On this healing journey we'll look at what we fear most—our rage, our shame, our grief—and allow it to be transformed instead of ignored. It's about becoming familiar with these quote, unquote "dark parts" of ourselves and developing a relationship with them. When we slowly invite these qualities to come up from within with curiosity and compassion, we can start to transform them. We get more comfortable with them instead of feeling rejected and shamed.

It's about the process of transforming your biggest wounds into light. Rumi said this best: "The wound is where the light enters." So where is your deepest wound? Look there and at least try to let the light enter. Because if you never look, that darkness will remain. It will always stay there, in the shadows. What you resist persists, my dear.

I'm gonna give it to you straight: This book doesn't exist to heal your inner wounds. It's not going to break your generational curses. It's not going to alchemize your shadow. I do not have the answers to all your problems. That's not what this book is for. That's the work for you to do after you read it, IF you chose to, as you go through the rest of your life.

I want you to see this book as an invitation to start tolerating the uncomfortable. You are cordially invited to face your shadow. Buckle in, kitty kats, because it's about to get real.

My personal hope is to introduce these concepts into your awareness so that, together, we can raise the collective consciousness. I'm not looking to be the next spiritual guru on the block or to be put on a pedestal. I am walking this complex human experience right beside you and sharing my perspective as we transform together.

I figure there are enough light workers on this planet already. With five Scorpio placements in my 10th house of career in my natal chart, of course I'm drawn to the shadow work. After all, the real gold is buried in the deepest mines of your psyche.

This book will show you how to stop rejecting the darkness inside of you and start integrating it into light, personal power, and wholeness. Darkness is not evil, it's the great void. Just like the inside of the womb, darkness can be an infinite source of your untapped potential and creativity. Or, as Carl Jung called it, your *shadow gold*.

So as you move forward, I ask you to meet this journey with curiosity, courage, and compassion.

For yourself.

For those who came before you.

And for the generations to come.

Let love flow where once there was only pain.

Ready or not, let's begin, my love.

Dr. Chahal

Part 1

THE SHADOW PRESCRIPTION

CHAPTER 1

CLUES IN DÉJÀ VU

Synchronicity is an ever present reality for those
who have eyes to see it.
–CARL JUNG

I don't know why, but Uber rides make me cry. It's happened so often when I've found myself driven to tears in the back of a cab that I figure it has to be something about the motion of the vehicle, sitting in the backseat and watching my life go by, that makes me finally stop running from the thoughts and feelings I usually avoid. Luckily, I've had so many kind and compassionate Uber and taxi drivers who check in and make sure I'm okay. At this point, I should start tipping extra for the emotional therapy. "Five stars for driving me, five stars for the emotional support."

So it wasn't much of a surprise to me when, about six months after I started Family Constellations, I got in an Uber to go get gelato, and I burst into tears, sobbing. As the car was driving me from Brooklyn to Manhattan, I found my mind wandering into my past. I started thinking about my teenage self and the first boyfriend I ever had. And out of nowhere, I started crying.

I wasn't crying for the guy. It wasn't like I was missing him. The tears were for me. I felt this overwhelming sense of who I was at 15. I could *feel* her, that girl I used to be. I could feel her fiery passion, her high functioning depression, and her deep insecurity. I could feel the intensely emotional nature of a girl navigating her first heartbreak while simultaneously distracting herself with books and burying her pain in academics. I could feel her independence fighting to break out of the unspoken rules of my lineage. I could feel every ounce of her pain rushing back into my body.

I pulled out my phone to text Meera, my Family Constellations practitioner. And out of all the things she could have asked me about my ex and what I was feeling, she responded, "The same guy who told you about your family history?"

Ding. Uffff.

Me crying in the back of this cab wasn't only an emotional wave passing through. This was synchronicity at play.

When I was 15, I was spitting venom at my ex after my ego got bruised from being dumped. I was *really* painting the town red and definitely not my proudest behavior in hindsight. (Hey, we listen and we don't judge. That's what the internet says, right?) Fed up with my drama, he finally retaliated by texting me: "Your great-grandmother killed your great-grandfather."

WHAT? I was raised by my grandmother from age 4 to 14 in Chandigarh, India shortly after my mother was diagnosed with schizophrenia after a suicide attempt. No one had ever mentioned this to me in my entire upbringing, so of course I ran to my grandmother to find out if it was true.

"This is a joke, right?" I asked, expecting her to tell me my ex was wrong. I wanted to hear, *Oh no! Of course your great-grandmother wasn't a murderer! What an outrageous thing to say!* But she didn't say that. Instead, she started sputtering about how her parents didn't get along, how her mother was from a very different family. And I just knew. My grandmother didn't have to confirm or deny anything; I knew from the look on her face that what my ex had said was true.

As a teenager, I wasn't spiritual or conscious of healing work, so I didn't process what learning this about my great-grandmother really meant. I was bombarded with this massive truth bomb and I wasn't given any tools to diffuse it. So I did what everyone in my family does when it comes to handling big, complicated emotions: I suppressed it down, deep into a box inside what I call the shadow cage—that place deep within my psyche where all the messy, painful feelings get locked away. Sweep, sweep, sweep under the rug it went. I tried to convince my logical brain that it didn't matter. She wasn't alive anymore so how could it still affect me or our family? It was all in the past, right?

Synchronicity isn't random; it's the soul's way of nudging us to deeper truths. It's divine orchestration. It's a circumstance or event that takes place, which you intuitively feel and know has not happened by mere chance. It's an inner knowing, even if it doesn't make logical sense. It's the mind's unconscious manifesting meaning into external reality.

As I sat on the faux leather seats in the back of that Uber car, reliving this period of my life, I realized my higher self was sending a giant neon sign pointed straight at my unresolved trauma.

I had experienced moments of déjà vu like this before, but this was the first time I truly recognized it for what it was. It was the start of the breadcrumb trail leading me down a path of deeper healing. A path that was about to dig up all the gunk buried within my teenage wounds and ancestral history. It was the synchronicity that told me everything I was feeling wasn't just about an ex or an old heartbreak. It was about me, my lineage, and the patterns I had inherited without realizing it.

SYNCHRONICITY IS NOT ALWAYS LOVE AND LIGHT

I used to think synchronicity was the cute, mystical version of coincidence. Like looking at the clock on the microwave at exactly 11:11, seeing 444 on a car's license plate, or thinking about an old friend you haven't spoken to in ages, and then they text you seemingly out of nowhere.

I used to think it was the kind of thing that makes you smile and think, *Wow, what are the odds?* But I quickly learned that synchronicity doesn't always show up as rainbows and unicorns or a gentle nudge from the Universe. Sometimes, if you have been ignoring those long enough, the freaking Universe yanks you by the hair and throws you headfirst into repeating painful patterns of your buried deepest wounds.

Similarly, when I first started Family Constellations, I thought, *Wow! This is like therapy on steroids!* I seriously thought I'd be able to bypass my own shadow work and heal without ever digging into the dark stuff. But that's not how this shit works. *Ugh!*

People often see synchronicity as a sign from the Universe that you're on the right track. That everything is hunkydory and nothing will ever go wrong. But synchronicity has another job too. It points you directly to the parts of yourself you've been avoiding. It's a cosmic highlighter marking the places where your wounds, fears, and unconscious patterns are running the show.

There's this expression that says you can't clean out a closet without pulling everything out first. Ignored long enough, the Universe will wrench open the doors, dump everything onto the floor, and make sure you can't ignore the mess anymore.

Before the synchronicities started showing up to point me to all the dark stuff I had to face, Meera warned me I'd be in for a rough ride. She told me that reentering the field was reopening a past trauma loop and it was extremely important to be trauma informed with this work.

At first, it was little things like feeling more emotional or getting triggered by conversations that normally wouldn't have bothered me. On the surface, these moments seemed inconsequential, but underneath they all showcased a single underlying theme. They were asking me to do the work, to make a change in my life. But I wasn't listening. So, then my body started reacting.

I developed insomnia, waking up at weird hours for no reason—not anxious, not thinking about anything—just awake. Then came the muscle twitching, very prominent, random twitches in different parts of my body. And then the worst part: My body started rejecting my old life.

I lost ten pounds in three weeks. I ended up in the ER. I had to fly to India to get an endoscopy because my stomach was burning in pain, and the doctors in the US kept telling me there was nothing wrong. In India, I learned I had an infection. My body was purging everything I put into it besides water. I remember sitting on the bathroom floor as my guts were spilling out of me, sobbing to one of my best friends on the phone, screaming at him that I was dying.

"I know," he said, way too calmly. "You are dying. This is a death."

I wasn't literally dying, although it could have become that serious if my body had started rejecting the water I was drinking too. My friend had seen this kind of spiritual death before. In another strange synchronicity, his life mirrored mine in many ways. He had also quit residency six months in, after going through his own dark night of the soul. We found each other through some random online app, two unraveling souls crossing paths at exactly the right time.

My body was purging a part of me that I no longer needed, and in that process, an old version of myself was dying. Purging my guts into the toilet was a way for my body to purge my past identities, trauma, and ancestral baggage that I had unconsciously carried for so long.

The solar plexus is the energetic center of personal power, drive, and ego identity. My solar plexus had been completely out of alignment for too long and that misalignment was manifesting as dis-ease in my body.

The body is so wise, if only we listened to its gentler nudges before it came to a point where you cannot ignore it any more. In Dr. Gabor Mate's phenomenal book, *When the Body Says No: The Cost of Hidden Stress*, he talks about if you don't say NO because you have been conditioned to play nice and not offend others, eventually your body will do it for you. Illness is your body drawing that boundary, screaming NO MORE. My soul was screaming at me to listen, and because I hadn't listened to any of the previous signs, the Universe decided to take drastic measures.

This was how my soul let me know it was time to quit my residency.

Had there been other signs before? Absolutely. I'd been feeling a deep sense of resistance to my work for a while. That was a sign. Conversations with friends, mentors, and even random people continuously had the theme of walking away. I started to resent my work. Another sign. The insomnia and muscle twitches? Yep, more signs. Had I listened to any of these signs? Nope. So the universe had to knock harder. It had to send more and more signs until I was vomiting on the floor in India and there was no way I could no longer not pay attention.

Synchronicity shows up when something inside us is ready to be seen, whether it's a belief, a wound, or an ancestral pattern that has been running in the background. It is trying to wake

27

you up to fulfill your destiny. Synchronicity is a mirror, a wake-up call, and sometimes a full-blown cosmic intervention.

In my case, it started subtly with a brief emotional breakdown in the back of an Uber or an inner knowing when reading a book. Then it got louder, and my body started purging, my life started breaking down, my dog went into heart failure, and the Universe forced me to look inward. The moment I signaled my readiness to transform, synchronicity accelerated in ways that felt overwhelming.

DEATH OMENS

If you don't address ancestral shadows (aka the trauma from your lineage) they don't go away. They get passed down. And if you don't heal it; your kids will have to. And if they don't, their kids will. Ancestral pain continues through generations unless someone actively chooses to confront and heal it.

My choice to confront and heal my family's ancestral shadows didn't happen overnight. It was through a period of repeated synchronicities that I realized this was the path my soul wanted. I kept seeing the same signs, the same patterns, the same wounds playing out in my own life.

The autumn after I left residency, I decided to go to Salem, Massachusetts on a whim.

I was watching a bad horror-comedy with a friend—one of those Halloween movies set in Salem. The plot was ridiculous, the jokes weren't landing, and about halfway through, I completely lost interest. But I couldn't lose this pull I was feeling to visit Salem. After all, why wasn't I going? It's Halloween. I had the time. I lived in Brooklyn, New York, so Boston was right there.

I didn't even wait for the credits to roll. I grabbed my phone and booked an Airbnb in Salem.

Then I packed my things, took my little witch hat I got off Etsy, and went.

And it was amazing. Salem was everything I wanted it to be; it was spooky, magical, and full of energy. I had the best time. But when I got back home, my apartment was infested with fruit flies.

I'm not talking about a few here and there, I mean hundreds of fruit flies covering my space like a biblical plague. There was one day where I spent six hours squashing flies all over my living room, jumping from one couch to another. I wanted to pull my hair out by the end of it.

They wouldn't leave. For two weeks, they tormented me. No matter what I did, how much I cleaned, how many traps I set, they kept multiplying. And somewhere deep in my gut, I knew this wasn't normal. This was an omen.

I brought it up to a close friend of mine who happens to be a practicing witch. She agreed it was an omen, but she didn't agree with me that it was a death omen. Still, the feeling wouldn't leave me alone. So I did what anyone with an internet connection and a sense of paranoia does. I googled it.

And there it was. Fruit flies represent transformation through death.

Not physical death. But an ego death. A spiritual death. A transformation was coming. And I knew, without a doubt, that it was coming for me.

Then, a few days later, I made my way on a preplanned trip to Mount Shasta in California, completely unaware that I was about to walk straight into the next chapter of my metamorphosis.

It was the night of Halloween, and I decided to pull a single Tarot card for myself. I sat in my Airbnb and shuffled the cards, focusing my intention into the deck. When I felt ready, I pulled a card and looked at it: Death. The damn Death card.

I stared at the card for a second, baffled. I thought, *What are the odds? Pulling the Death card on All Hallows' Eve?* Again, I clocked the card pull as an omen, but I still didn't understand what it meant. Two death omens in two weeks? That's got to mean something, right?

I also noted the significance of the date. Not only was it Halloween, a holiday that originated from the Celtic tradition of Samhain, a day when spirits were said to walk the earth, but it was also close to Día de los Muertos, the Latin American holiday that celebrated the same thing—the day of honoring the dead. Not to mention it was the New Moon in Scorpio, which signals a time for change and transformation. It's pretty easy to argue that death itself fits under that umbrella.

Two death omens in two weeks and the second one was a doozy of a synchronicity with all the corresponding dates. The Universe was definitely trying to tell me something. I just didn't know what.

Mount Shasta is the root chakra of the earth. If you're familiar with the chakra system, you may know that the root chakra represents survival, security, safety, and literally our roots (i.e., ancestral roots). I went there to get a blessing from the mountain and from Mother Earth. After leaving my residency, my life was essentially starting over. As I started this new chapter in my life, I wanted to visit the mountain to help me feel rooted in my purpose.

I thought I was going there to connect with divine energy and receive blessings for my next chapter in life. I saw it as a spiritual pilgrimage in a place where I could tap into higher wisdom and gain a deeper understanding of myself.

While I was there, I thought it would be fun to do this Eulogy spell I'd learned from my witchy friend. I picked the perfect spot on the mountain, next to a waterfall, and buried a piece of my hair into the ground. Then, I recited, "Here lies the body of Meher, the girl who used to people-please and chase for love, and work so hard to prove her femininity, and…" Blah, blah, blah. I described the version of myself I wanted to let go of in detail. I followed the instructions of the spell, called in the four directions, and felt like such a badass witch. I was like, *Look at me! I'm so witchy! So much fun for my inner child to be casting spells!*

The ritual was symbolic of my transition. I didn't think it was *that* serious. It didn't really occur to me that I was standing on a mountain known for being a spiritual energy vortex, a few days after I pulled the Death card on Halloween, performing an actual *eulogy* for myself.

This eulogy was amplified by the ancestral portals that had just opened. A eulogy that was amplified by my sincere intentions of healing and transition. Not to mention amplified by the powerful energy of majestic Mount Shasta itself.

It wasn't until months later that I realized the impact of what I had done. I'd put a literal death spell on myself. I'd performed the ritual as a way to consciously grieve, honor, and release my past self. It was a moment of acknowledging my wounds, seeing them for what they were, and choosing to move forward. But it also acted as a portal, and a PURGE. It was a ritual severance from the unconscious patterns that had been running in my family for generations. It was my energetic agreement to dig up the shit from my past and end the cycle of trauma for myself and the future generations of my lineage. Eulogy spells are definitely not for the faint of heart, and it was a pretty rough experience for me. I don't recommend this, dear reader, if you have a lot of unprocessed trauma.

The root chakra is the chakra of survival. It's also where you store the emotion of fear and trauma, and it's the chakra that connects you to your ancestors. That spell, the Tarot pull, and the flies, the news from my brother, which I mention ahead, were all synchronicities from the Universe letting me know it was time to heal my family's past. It was up to me to alchemize my ancestral shadows.

THE WAKE UP CALL

The next day while still in Shasta I decided to spend the day inside instead of touristing the cute town because it was heavily pouring outside. I called my brother from my Airbnb and I was on a video call with him when, in the most casual way possible, he mentioned, "You know, we're famous in history because of our great grandma."

I blinked. "What do you mean, famous in history?"

"Come on, you know this."

I did not, in fact, know this. Sure, thanks to my ex, I knew what happened. I knew that everyone in the town where I grew up knew about my family's past. But that's small towns for you, everybody knows everybody. Everybody talks. But famous? Like, actually famous?

"Meher, it's in history books. This was a Supreme Court of India case."

My 17-year-old brother said it like it was nothing, like he was commenting on the weather. But I couldn't breathe. The Supreme Court. The highest court in India. This wasn't some local scandal that faded with time; this was a case that had literally shaped Indian law around legal evidence in murder.

The story I thought was safely hidden away in my family's skeleton closet was being taught in India to kids in history class and soon-to-be lawyers in law school. They were learning about my great-grandmother, the blood of my blood as an example of a section in the constitution modified. As I processed what he was telling me, my legs went cold as if they'd been dunked in a bucket of ice water. I was carrying this woman's DNA in my womb. *Are you fucking kidding me?*

My brother sent me a YouTube link to a video by a history teacher with over 250,000 followers. The title of the video was my great-grandmother's name, versus the State of India and it had thousands of views. You know, no big deal, just another casual Friday.

When I clicked play, I saw my family's darkest trauma play out on the screen: my great-grandmother and great-grandfather played by stick figures, like it was a true crime episode. There it was—her trial, how the murder happened, how her husband's body was found in a well two months later because the water supply got contaminated from decomposition.

Jesus Christ.

For two whole months, the police could not find him.

I gripped my phone. My hands were shaking. I could not finish the whole video.

This was the sort of story that belonged in a Netflix crime documentary. It was the kind of story associated with the Menendez brothers, rather than a typical family like mine.

I have this DNA in me. I have this DNA in me.

It was the only thought looping through my head. Of course this had to happen on the Scorpio New Moon, this divine synchronicity, receiving this knowledge about my roots in the root chakra of the world, sent from the other side, when the veil was thin on Halloween.

THE TRAUMA IN MY BLOOD

I called Meera. And barely able to get the words out, I told her what I had just learned. Her response was immediate:

"Oh my God, Meher. Are you okay? Are you safe right now?"

Safe? How do you answer a question like that when your entire body is screaming that you're not?

She told me to get in a bath, to ground myself, and to let the water regulate my nervous system. Epsom salt. Hot water. Let it ground you.

And it worked. Water is the most feminine element, the element of emotions. It holds memory. It heals. But even as I soaked in the bath, trying to breathe through the shock, I knew this was just the beginning. I am so grateful to this element for holding sacred space for all my emotions in my dark night of the soul.

"Meher," she told me, "this is significant. Not just because someone was murdered, not only because your grandmother became an orphan at six months old, but because this trauma never got processed. And it didn't just stay in your family, it was so public on a national level. This is a whole other level of ancestral trauma."

She was right. This wasn't only a private family wound; it was a public humiliation that had never been acknowledged or grieved properly. And now, decades later, the weight of it was still moving through me. The women after her, including my grandmother, mother, and myself had spent our entire lives unconsciously carrying something I never even knew existed.

RHYME OF DIVINE TIME

Synchronicity is not exclusive to certain people; it happens to everybody, every day. You, reading this book right now, could be a synchronicity.

Something led you to pick up this book, whether it was something about the title that resonated with you, a friend recommended it to you, or you stumbled across it and felt a certain pull to flip through the pages. Whatever the reason, this book could be a synchronistic breadcrumb leading you toward your larger journey.

And don't worry, while synchronicities aren't always love and light, they're not always as deep or traumatic as the story I shared above. I mean, with my six Scorpio placements in my natal chart, it's pretty clear my higher self was like, *Let's pick this bitch to bring light to the deep, dark waters only the scorpion is willing to swim through.* Now I understand why depth has been such a driving force for me in my personal life.

But if the Universe is sending you synchronicities, then that begs the question: Are you paying attention?

The Universe is always speaking. Through patterns. Through symbols. Through the same lessons showing up over and over again in different disguises. Maybe you've noticed them before but brushed them off. Maybe you've had a gut feeling that something wasn't just a coincidence but never stopped to ask why.

This is your invitation to start noticing.

Take a moment to reflect:

- Have you noticed repeating symbols, numbers, people, or experiences that feel strangely connected?
- Do certain challenges, emotional wounds, or family patterns seem to keep replaying in your life? (These are

known as hidden loyalties in the language of systemic/ family constellations.)

- Have you ever met someone who felt destined to cross your path—as if they were there to teach you something?
- Has life ever forced you to slow down, shift directions, or face something you were trying to avoid?

These aren't just coincidences. These are breadcrumbs. They're road signs leading you toward deeper healing.

So start observing. Don't overthink it. Just notice. The patterns that once repeated can end with you. The wounds that went unacknowledged are finally seen. The story that has been playing out for generations gets the opportunity to be rewritten. That's why they say history repeats itself. Your soul will keep knocking until it gets so loud you are left with no choice but to listen.

And, if you're like I was and think you're one of the lucky ones who got this far without having trauma.... Well, here's a newsflash for you: Every single one of us has trauma. That's just part of the human experience incarnating on this planet.

Trauma isn't only the big, obvious, movie-worthy events. It's also the small, quiet ways we learned to disconnect from ourselves to survive. It shapes our past, present, and future. If we don't face it and work our way through it, it shows up in our relationships, our fears, our ability to trust, our ability to receive, and our ability to be seen.

So, if you've ever wondered, Why do I feel like something is off, even though my life looks fine on paper? If you've ever minimized your pain because someone else had it worse. If you've ever been told to be grateful instead of acknowledging what hurt you…

Then you're exactly where you need to be.

And in the next chapter, we're going to talk about that.

CHAPTER 2

THE TRAUMA FREE FANTASY

When an inner situation is not made conscious, it appears
outside as fate.
–CARL JUNG

So, you don't think you have trauma? Let's talk about that.

First of all, if it serves you to think you're trauma-free, I'm not here to burst your bubble. This is a planet of free will. If you were drawn to this book, you likely have at least some awareness of wounds.

Maybe you picked up this book because you're just a little curious about healing and self-awareness. Maybe you're spiritually inclined and want to learn more about shadow work. You know, just for educational purposes. Perhaps you can feel there is something off, but you just can't put your finger on it.

But *YOU* certainly don't have *TRAUMA*. At least, not the capital-T, soul-sucking, underworld-level kind of trauma, right?

After all, maybe you grew up in a nice house. Perhaps your parents stayed together. You might have been praised all your life for being "the mature one" or "resilient," the type of person who could handle anything life threw at them. You've likely built yourself a successful life, or you're currently building one. You've heard horror stories from friends and family who really have experienced trauma, and you're so grateful nothing like that has ever happened to you.

On the surface, everything looks great. And yet, here you are. Because something still feels... off. Sometimes you feel overwhelmed or disconnected. Or overreact to "small" things. And then the thought creeps in: *What's wrong with me?*

Well, first of all, there is *nothing* wrong with you. And second, everybody has trauma in some shape or form. We haven't all experienced trauma in a way that leads to a trauma disorder diagnosis, thank Goddess. But even if your horrors aren't newsworthy, there are still events that have happened throughout your life that caused stress. And even if you won the lottery of all lotteries and have lived a life fully free of any traumatic incidents, trauma isn't just about what happened to you. It's also about what *didn't* happen.

It's not always the car crash or the screaming match or the slap across the face. Sometimes it's the silence. The absence of soothing. The feeling of invisibility. For instance, so much of my trauma actually comes from the fact that my mother just couldn't attune to me or co-regulate with me due to her illness.

For the longest time, I didn't think I had any trauma either. I mean I was a doctor right? Many people deny their trauma, not out of arrogance, but out of instinct. Denial is a built-in protective mechanism. It's a protective layer against experiencing that pain again. Its battlecry is 'ignorance is bliss.' What you don't remember can't hurt you again. Or maybe you went to a school, or grew up in a community where all of it was normalised.

Except that's not exactly true. Yes, the defense mechanism protected you. It was a coping strategy in your childhood, your teenage years, maybe even your first job. But eventually, it stops working. It begins to manifest externally until you can't ignore it anymore. Until one day you realize you have to open Pandora's box. Denial works until it doesn't. And when it stops, the shadow doesn't just live inside you anymore…it starts spilling into your outer world.

WHAT IS TRAUMA, REALLY?

We tend to associate trauma with the obvious: abuse, violence, loss, death, war. The kind of things that leave physical marks or make headlines. But trauma isn't always loud or visible. And it's not always what happened. Nearly as often, it's the lack of something. The lack of love, protection, validation, or boundaries can leave emotional scars. It causes deep soul wounding and fragmentation.

Trauma is any experience, or lack of experience, that causes you deep emotional distress. It's any event or experience which exceeds your nervous system and your body's ability to regulate itself at that time.

When your body perceives a threat—real or imagined—it goes into a protective state: fight, flight, freeze, or fawn. That's your survival system kicking in, thanks to millions of years of human evolution. But if your nervous system can't switch off after the threat has passed, the trauma stays lodged in your body. It keeps looping, silently shaping your emotions, decisions, and patterns.

Trauma is also deeply subjective, which is why two people can experience the same event and be affected in completely different ways. Even siblings raised in the same household may carry very different imprints of what happened while they were growing up. For example, both siblings may have experienced being slapped or beaten at the same time, but their responses may vary dramatically.

One might have had someone there to soothe them, to help them process what happened. The other might have had no one. Even if both of them had the same form of regulation afterwards, each person's own experience is unique to them. That difference alone changes everything.

Trauma doesn't only depend on the event; it depends on what happened afterward and whether the nervous system could return to a sense of safety. Even when animals are threatened, they instinctively shake to discharge that energy. But when we don't get to tap into our internal Taylor Swift and "shake it off, shake it off," that stress stays trapped in the body. Remember how we spoke about EMOTION equaling energy in motion? Trauma is this energy trapped and still looping in your body even after significant time has passed.

And it's not just what happens after the trauma; it's everything that came before it too. The way your nervous system was shaped, the support you had access to, the family system you were born into, cultural and religious contexts of dealing with those things all influence how trauma lands in your body.

Maybe the older sibling had inexperienced parents who didn't know how to regulate or respond. By the time the second child came along, the parents had matured or learned from their mistakes. One might carry more of the mother's emotional sensitivity; the other could have inherited a tendency toward physical illness. In later chapters we dive deeper in family constellation work but, broadly speaking, inherited trauma is more pronounced from the same sex parent. Female progeny inherit more of the maternal lineage trauma and male progeny of their father's side.

It's more than the trauma; it's the whole internal and external landscape that determines how deeply these experiences are felt.

These nuances matter.

It's important to practice self-compassion and to not compare your pain to someone else's. There will always be someone who has experienced something worse than you have. But that doesn't mean your pain doesn't matter. That's how you get stuck in the trauma Olympics and start focusing your energy on trying to prove that your wounds are worthy of attention. I've definitely fallen into that trap, believing that my mother's illness was worse than anyone else's. That mindset gave me a kind of victim entitlement that kept me stuck. I still struggle with it at times, and I practice letting go of the need to be "perfectly" healed from this.

Not everyone's trauma looks the same. It exists across a wide spectrum of human experience, and every experience is real and valid.

You may have heard of *Big T* and *little T* as terms used to delineate levels of trauma. Big T refers to the obvious events: physical abuse, sexual assault, car accidents, war, witnessing violence, sudden loss. While little T refers to the quieter wounds: emotional neglect, parentification, chronic invalidation, subtle but repeated experiences of not being seen, soothed, or protected. Honestly, I don't like this differentiation. Who decides what is Big T and little T anyways?

And while the terms Big T and little T may seem like one is worse than the other, that's not always the case. A study highlighted by the American Psychological Association found that children who are emotionally abused and neglected face similar and sometimes worse mental health problems compared to those who are physically or sexually abused.[7] From personal experience, I know there is a deep pain which comes when our gifts are not cherished, valued, or seen.

---

7 American Psychological Association. (2014, October 28). Psychological abuse is as harmful as other types of child abuse. https://www.apa.org/news/press/releases/2014/10/psychological-abuse.

Neglect is deeply, deeply painful. That kind of unworthiness stays with us, in our shadow, wherever you go.

I once asked Meera how people with so much trauma are able to accomplish so much despite tons of excruciating life experiences. They become presidents, leaders, doctors, CEOs. *Like, how?* What she told me in response to this really struck a chord: "Trauma either kills you or makes you superhuman." Damn that's so true.

You don't need to check a box that says "trauma victim" to know you've been impacted. If your nervous system got overwhelmed and couldn't reset, that was trauma. If you had to adapt to survive by shrinking, pleasing, hiding, staying silent, that was trauma. If you felt invisible, unworthy, or too much, guess what? That was trauma. You can't heal what you refuse to acknowledge.

INHERITED WOUNDS: THE SHADOWS THAT AREN'T EVEN YOURS

Here's where it gets even wilder: Most of the trauma you're carrying may not even be yours. It is my personal opinion that more than 90% of the trauma lodged in your cells and body is not primarily yours. It is deeply ancestral.

That heaviness in your chest, the people-pleasing pattern you can't break, the unexplained guilt that shows up every time you choose yourself. Some of that might belong to an ancestor you've never even met, like your grandfather who may carry the guilt of killing people in war or a sibling who was aborted. Someone whose energy still lives inside your family line.

For example, in the 1950s, my great-grandmother murdered my great-grandfather. It happened long before I was born, when my grandma was still an infant. And yet, I still carry the trauma from my family's history because my family never fully processed the event before I came along.

This is where Family Constellations and ancestral shadow work come in. If those terms are new to you, don't worry. You're about to get an intimate understanding of what they mean and how they can help you transform the unconscious patterns you've been carrying, often without even realizing it.

Family Constellations works with the Orders of Love. Trauma is seen as a break in this love bond within the family system. It's something that lives in the energetic field of a family and is passed down through generations like an invisible heirloom. It also manifests in interrupted movements, like an infant separated from their mother at birth. The infant cries and tries to reach out for the mother, but she isn't there. This can show up as a lifelong pattern of learned helplessness. Birth history is also significant from an FC perspective. When one person isn't given the right to belong—in other words, when the correct order is disrupted—another family member or descendant may become entangled in the empty space that's created. What gets silenced in one generation often finds a voice in the next. The systemic field always seeks balance and order. Often, without even realizing it, we inherit our ancestors' unresolved pain: their shame, their secrets, their survival patterns. And we unconsciously act them out as a way to belong. The field doesn't care about personal morality; it cares about restoring greater equilibrium.

In Family Constellations, the aim is to step back into the field and close this trauma loop so that love can flow and be restored in the system. The field is not biased, and nonjudgmental. In the field, both the victim and perpetrator have an equal right to belong. We often place judgment on perpetrators thinking that moral superiority entitles us to belong more. But this is not the case.

Sometimes, this unconscious loyalty to your family system shows up as hidden dynamics in the same patterns as the generations that came before: attracting emotionally unavailable partners, eating disorders, underearning despite being talented, and feeling emotionally responsible for everyone else. It might also look like physical illness, unexplained anxiety, or an inability to move forward in life, no matter how much healing work you've already done.

From the Family Constellation perspective, a lot of the trauma that you carry in your body or on your soul level doesn't even belong to you. You're carrying it for your ancestors.

I mean that literally. It's not a metaphor. Science is starting to catch up with what spiritual traditions have known for centuries. Studies in epigenetics have shown that traumatic experiences can alter gene expression, switching microRNAs in DNA on and off and those changes can be passed down to future generations.

What this could mean for you is that your great-grandmother's grief of child loss could be part of the reason you carry so much sadness. Your grandfather's war trauma could be part of why you're always bracing for disaster.

One study found that individuals who experienced childhood trauma showed measurable epigenetic changes in genes related to stress regulation and emotional resilience. These changes were also observed in their children, who had not experienced the original trauma themselves.[8] This means that emotional pain and survival adaptations can leave a biological imprint, one that echoes down the family line.

So no, it's not all in your head. And no, you're not broken. You're just carrying more than your share. Maybe you're here because you're ready to set some of it down. Working with the field has taught me a lot of humility, which science could not. It has humbled my intellect, which always tries to dissect and conclude an answer. Such is the human ego.

Bert Hellinger is known as the father of constellations. He used to hold workshops between the Jewish victims and Nazi soldiers, both parties who suffered from severe PTSD, to bring healing and restore balance. I have a lot of respect for Hellinger. I think being a Catholic German priest and psychotherapist by vocation was quite bold and ahead of his time. After serving in World War II, he travelled to Africa in the hope of finding healing for his own traumas from experiencing the bloodshed. He came across the Zulu tribe who helped him and also taught him this ancestral medicine of Family Constellations. He then brought this medicine back to Europe, incorporating into his psychotherapeutic interventions and helped several people heal with these workshops.

---

8 N. Perroud, et al. (2025), Epigenetic modifications associated with childhood trauma and adult psychopathology: Evidence for transmission across generations. *Scientific Reports*, 15, Article 89818, https://www.nature.com/articles/s41598-025-89818-z.

Hellinger stated, "To gain insight into the Orders of Love is wisdom; to follow them with love is humility." Hellinger dedicated his life's work to understanding the hidden dynamics of family systems and the unconscious loyalties that shape our lives. His legacy invites us to look beyond surface-level explanations and embrace the deeper truths that move in the family soul. The language of science demands a precision that doesn't always reach the soul. Family Constellations invites us to feel, to sense, to experience, and to know in our bones what belongs, what doesn't, and what longs to be integrated.

Before this comes across as me selling FC as the next magic pill and cure to all your problems, I want to add an *extremely* important disclaimer: Systemic and Family Constellation can be retraumatising. I'm going to bring up FC a lot throughout this book because it has been a transformational modality for me. However, I want to be clear when I say, FC healing workshops and one-on-one sessions involve going back into the past and stepping in for your ancestors to find the source of a pain. When you do this, you may uncover very dark and traumatic truths.

This is beyond the grasp of the conscious mind and is why I can not stress enough how important it is to work with a practitioner who is trauma informed and can hold space for your nervous system to metabolize this traumatic energy. Hellinger received a lot of backlash in his career at a later stage for retraumatising sexual abuse victims to face their perpetrator too soon or too quickly in the field. When it comes to shadow work, slow and steady is the name of the game. Please give your nervous system time to integrate and don't push yourself for early resolutions if you are not ready. A small and right amount of poison can act like medicine but the same poison ingested in large quantities too soon can be dangerous.

So, take a breath. This is A LOT to take in. As you keep reading, remember to come back to your breath if you need to ground yourself. The next layer we're about to explore is the very thing that's kept so many of us from seeing our pain clearly in the first place.

Denial as Defense Mechanism and Collective Gaslighting Around Trauma

Let's be real: No one wants to see themselves as a victim. It feels powerless. Defeated. Uncomfortable. In a world that celebrates strength, productivity, and positivity, victimhood is often treated like a dirty word.

Sometimes the refusal to acknowledge our trauma isn't about arrogance. It's about protection. It's the mind and body trying to spare us from pain we didn't have the tools to process at the time.

And for a while, it works. You get good at surviving. You push the feelings down, stay productive, and keep going. You become the strong one. The reliable one. The overachiever. Society rewards that. But at some point, the cracks start to show. The coping strategy that once saved you starts to sabotage you. You burn out. You shut down. Your body starts breaking down, or your relationships do. And suddenly, you find yourself in a therapist's office asking: "What the hell is happening to me?"

Sometimes it's easier to cling to the belief that you're "fine" than to confront the reality of what you survived. When your life looks good on paper, it's tempting to ignore what's underneath, especially if you've been told that privilege and pain can't coexist.

But the truth is: You can be privileged and still carry deep wounds. You can be smart, successful, spiritual, *and* still be in denial about your trauma.

When your life looks good on paper, society loves to double down on the denial for you. Enter: collective gaslighting. All the well-meaning (and not-so-well-meaning) voices around you saying, "You're fine. What do you have to be upset about?"

Maybe you've heard it. Maybe you've said it to yourself:

You were rich, so it couldn't have been that bad.

You had food. You went to a good school. You had parents who stayed together. Why are you complaining?

Just be grateful for what you have.

Oh my goddess, I hate that last one. Nobody consciously chooses to be ungrateful. The so-called "ungratefulness" comes from unprocessed pain and trauma that block the ability to feel genuine gratitude.

These phrases are a form of gaslighting that society at large is programmed to repeat. These messages are meant to shut you down and further add to shame spirals. And often, they work.

I grew up rich and I'm not ashamed to say it. But I used to be. In fact, the times in my life when I was the most suicidal came from shame around money. I used to think there was something defective in me that despite being financially secure, I was still so unhappy.

When you have even an ounce of privilege, society expects you to be happy, no matter what. And if you struggle with depression, it feels shameful because you "should be grateful for what you have." I felt like I had to hide my depression, because otherwise people would think that I was spoiled. The shame enveloped me like a big, ugly, weighted blanket. I felt like I had no right to feel the sadness I was feeling.

When someone tells you to be happy with what you have and ignore the aspects that are upsetting you, it creates a sense of deep shame around emotions that are actually perfectly normal and human. It's not helpful. It darkens your shadow.

There's a quote I love from the actor Jim Carrey that says, "I wish everyone could get rich and famous and everything they ever dreamed of so they can see that's not the answer."

Money, fame, and success are no substitute for healing the pain at your root.

Feeling something doesn't require permission. There is no prerequisite requiring you to be oppressed enough to feel a certain way. Feeling doesn't ask for your bank account, your body type, or your accomplishments. When someone tells you not to feel what you're feeling, it doesn't make the feeling go away, especially when you tell yourself that. It just buries it deeper.

"Just be grateful" might sound like good advice. But more often than not, it's a way of avoiding discomfort, both yours and theirs. It's spiritual bypassing 101.

Pain is pain. And if you feel it, it's real. Period.

THE SHAME CAGE: WHY ACKNOWLEDGING TRAUMA FEELS SO HARD

Even once you've begun to see your trauma for what it is, something else usually shows up hot on its heels: *shame.* It's an innocent emotion trying to keep you small, safe, and belonging to those around you.

The shame cage is where all the parts of you you've been told are too much, too needy, too messy, or too emotional go to hide. It's where your truth gets locked away, because somewhere along the way, you learned that being real could cost you belonging.

We do this without even realizing it. You start to feel shame and, instinctively, you shove it down. You fawn. You freeze. You smile when you want to scream. You swallow the lump in your throat. Because if you show what's really going on, someone might judge you. Or even worse, they might leave you.

But shame is not your fault. Shame was put there by society, by culture, by your family system. This is nobody's fault. It is a perpetuating cycle. It was installed like a glitchy app in your operating system that's constantly telling you you're doing life wrong.

That need to belong is real. We all want to be loved. We all want to be chosen. So we silence ourselves. We twist into versions of who we think we need to be in order to be accepted. And when we do that long enough, we lose track of who we actually are.

Shame doesn't just keep us "safe." It also keeps us stuck. And for many of us, especially women, shame has been used like a leash. To keep us small. To keep us agreeable. To keep us "pretty" and palatable and out of the way.

I've felt this firsthand. I once posted a photo of myself on Instagram where my cleavage was visible, nothing outrageous, just a photo that made me feel radiant and alive. I loved how I looked in the photo. I loved the dress I wore and how sexy I felt in it. But not even an hour later, I was bombarded with messages from women in my own family begging me to take it down. My grandmother cried. My aunt said, "Why do you want to be the talk of the town? Do you want wagging tails around you?"

Suddenly, my joy became something shameful.

Let that sink in: My cleavage made her cry.

If this had happened five years earlier, I probably would've taken it down. I would've apologized and folded into myself, retreating from my authenticity to keep the peace, like I'd done a hundred times before. The cost of obedience became too high.

And that's the work. This is the healing. Not to avoid shame, but to stop letting it run your life.

To look into that shame cage and ask: Who put this here? Why did I believe it? And do I still want to carry it?

Because once you start to see shame for what it really is—not a reflection of your unworthiness, but a byproduct of conditioning—you begin to set yourself free.

The Unseen Burden: Emotional Neglect and Parentification

By now, you probably realize that trauma isn't always about *what* happened. Sometimes it's about what *never* happened. One of the most invisible, overlooked forms of trauma is emotional neglect.

You weren't hit. You weren't screamed at. But no one ever asked how you were doing. No one noticed your sadness. No one taught you how to regulate your nervous system or how to make sense of your feelings. You were left to figure it out on your own, and that silence carved just as deep as any wound. This is often how avoidant attachment style is formed in childhood.

This is also where we begin to understand something called parentification. It's a term that sounds clinical, but for many of us, defines the reality of our entire childhood.

Parentification happens when a child is forced to become the emotional caretaker of a parent. Expected to be the one who holds it together, the child grows up fast. They become hyperaware of the parent's moods, editing their own emotions to avoid rocking the boat. Aunts, uncles, grandparents, and every neighbor with an opinion nod approvingly, "She's so mature for her age." But this is not a compliment; it's the sad reality of a child who never got to be a child. Too busy anticipating the next meltdown or focused on keeping the peace, there's little space left to figure out what they themselves truly need.

It's not a conscious choice; it's a survival response. When you grow up like this, who you really are at your core gets buried. You're trained to betray yourself to keep everyone else regulated. Your sadness becomes dangerous. Your anger becomes shameful. Your needs become invisible, even to you.

But the feelings don't disappear. They just get buried deeper. And buried emotions always find a way to resurface, through illness, burnout, anxiety, depression, cancer, or worse.

From a Family Constellation perspective, parentification is doomed to fail for both parties. It's the wrong order of love. Life force energy can not flow upwards from child to parent at least not when you are little. As a parentified eldest daughter, I have wept several times, still grieving in layers that I ultimately cannot save my mother from her illness.

This is a childlike superhero innocence, the belief that *I can save the world, I can save my parents from their fate.* It's not stupidity. It's innocent and pure love.

So if you were the "calm one," the "mature one," the "rock of the family," it might be time to ask yourself: Who asked you to be that? What did you have to give up to play that role? And what would it look like to finally put it down?

BREAKING FREE: THE PROCESS OF ALCHEMIZING TRAUMA

So, you're probably wondering, how do we actually heal?

Well, we certainly don't heal by bypassing our shadow. It doesn't happen from reframing it into something "positive." We don't simply package our trauma into a pretty affirmation and pretend it's over.

I'm talking about real healing.

It's the kind that unhooks generational trauma from your nervous system. The kind that rewires your inner world so you stop running the same painful patterns. The kind that leaves you raw but free.

This is what I call shadow alchemy.

It's the process of turning your deepest pain into embodied wisdom. Of facing what you've buried. Of grieving what you never received. Of reclaiming the parts of yourself you had to abandon just to survive.

It's not cute. It's not linear. And it's definitely not easy.

Sometimes, alchemy looks like sitting on the floor of your bedroom sobbing because you finally admitted to yourself that your parents couldn't love you the way you needed them to. Sometimes it's rage. Sometimes it's screaming in the shower. Sometimes it's numbness. Sometimes it's silence that stretches for weeks. Sometimes it's reverting back to old unhealthy coping mechanisms. And that's okay. But eventually, there is a mellowing.

You slowly stop chasing approval. You stop performing. You stop begging the world to love you the way your inner child still aches for, and you learn to give that love to yourself.

This is how you reclaim your power.

It's not about "getting over it." It's about getting *under* it so you can feel it, metabolize it, and let it go.

It's about shining a light on the shadow so it stops running the show in your life.

This isn't just about you. This is about the people who come after you. This is about the generations before you who didn't have the chance to heal.

This is about breaking the cycle.

And because you're here, reading this, peeking into the dark, you're already doing it.

So, take a breath. You've made it through the myth of a trauma-free life. Now, let's talk about the systems that keep that myth alive and how to start trusting your body again.

CHAPTER 3

SHADOW PSYCHIATRY

Neurosis is always a substitute for legitimate suffering.
–CARL JUNG

There are many moments I will never forget from when I worked in the psychiatric ward and emergency room . It's not easy to shut out memories of strapping someone onto a patient bed and injecting them with medication, forcefully restraining them with straps and drugs so they can't hurt anyone, including themselves. That's not something you can easily obliviate from your memory, especially when it's so frequent.

But what was even more difficult than restraining adults was when a child was put under my charge. There's nothing quite like the helplessness of looking into a child's eyes and being told by your superior to diagnose them with bipolar disorder at age 14. My heart would ache for them when they opened in interviews about their sexual abuse, about how their single mom is away to work, they are so lonely, and being bullied at school. This wasn't a psychiatric problem, this was a lack of love, affection, attention, and care.

I remember sitting in front of a 6-year-old and being expected to slap on a diagnosis. Oppositional defiant disorder, attention-deficit/hyperactivity disorder (ADHD), intermittent explosive disorder. Maybe all three. The child hadn't even lost all their baby teeth, and yet the system wanted to label them, medicate them, and move on. Are you kidding me? He's 6 years old. I didn't want him to have a huge portfolio of diagnosis before he became an adult and faced the real world.

I often met with children who had clear developmental challenges, and yet they were being labeled with schizophrenia. Did they have schizophrenia? Not likely. But the medication for schizophrenia would calm their behavioral outbursts. That was the logic:If the meds worked, the label stuck. And so, just like that, a child with an intellectual disability would be stamped with a psychiatric diagnosis that didn't belong to them. The system needed a reason to prescribe the drugs. Without that label, the residential facility would not accept the child back until the child had been reevaluated for the tenth time for a behavioral outburst.

In medical school, we're taught that psychiatry is a science. We memorize the *Diagnostic and Statistical Manual of Mental Disorders Fifth Edition* (DSM-5) criteria published by the American Psychiatric Association, learn the medications, and follow the evidence. But what they don't teach us, what no textbook can prepare us for, is what it feels like to be complicit in a system that restrains adults, injects them into sedation, and calls it wellness. It's easy to fall asleep, to follow the herd, to trust the authorities without question. But when we pause and ask why—why memorize a manual that, in its third edition, classified being gay as a mental disorder? We start to see the cracks. Even science is not immune to the prejudices of its time. The DSM is a tool, but it's not the truth. And so the real question becomes: Who decides what counts as a disorder, and whose voices are left out?

I became a doctor because I wanted to help people. Okay, sure, it also satisfied my ego by granting me that societal stamp of approval and respect, and I was feeding into the huge psychological burden of the unfulfilled desires of my parents. But underneath all of that, in my soul, I've always felt I'm here for a bigger purpose. My desire is to help heal and support individuals through their struggles. I want to make a meaningful impact in people's lives and help them alchemize their pain. But during my residency, I didn't feel like I was making the type of difference I knew I could.

Instead I felt chained and resentful. My work felt superficial. There was no depth to what we were doing and no one was getting better. No matter how many times I showed up, no matter how many protocols I followed, the outcomes didn't change and the suffering didn't ease.

We can learn 500 different genes involved in the stress response. We can cite every methylated RNA and every genetic marker linked to mental illness. But if someone's standing in front of us in crisis, none of that matters. They don't care about our textbook knowledge. They just want help.

Would you not want to punch someone if you were in excruciating pain in the hospital and they started giving you the logical workings of different nerves in your body?

At some point, I had to ask myself: What's more important? Showing off how brilliant you are by reciting obscure data? Or actually helping someone—getting to the root cause of why they're hurting and actually fixing the problem? Which is the greatest service we can offer as healers? I started to realize that all the textbook knowledge in the world means nothing if it can't actually help the person sitting right in front of us.

The more I practiced, the more dissonance I felt. I started to learn that institutional psychiatry wasn't about healing, it's about managing symptoms just enough to stay on schedule, satisfy billing codes, and keep the system running. It's a network of good intentioned people who want to help but who are stuck in a system that prevents thorough investigation. It's the illusion of care.

And I couldn't do it anymore. I started to see blood on my hands. Now you could not pay me a billion dollars to incorrectly diagnose a little kid. That is what I see as blood money. My soul's integrity won't allow it.

THE SHADOW SIDE OF WESTERN PSYCHIATRY

Once I saw the flaws in the system, I couldn't unsee them. Psychiatry wasn't broken because of bad doctors, it was broken because the system was built to move quickly. It was built to sedate pain, not to understand the root and heal the cause.

Western psychiatry, as it stands now, is obsessed with the surface. It fixates on symptoms. What can we see? What's loud and visible? It rarely asks what those symptoms are trying to say. Someone comes in depressed, and we're trained to match the checklist, pick the diagnosis, and prescribe the pill. We're trained to treat the branches, not the root.

One of the most frustrating tools in the entire system is the *Diagnostic and Statistical Manual of Mental Disorders* aka the DSM. It's this giant tome of a book that's basically looked at as the bible of psychiatry. It's the reference book doctors use for diagnosing and classifying mental disorders. But what most people don't realize is that it was never designed for healing because it was created for billing.

That's right. The book your psychiatrist will use to determine if you actually do suffer from depression or anxiety was developed to help insurance companies categorize symptoms so they could reimburse clinicians. Over time, it morphed into a diagnostic weapon used to define identities, assign lifelong labels, and force people into rigid boxes that often don't reflect their lived experience.

It's not that diagnoses are inherently harmful. Sometimes they're helpful. But when a person's entire complexity is reduced to a billing code, we lose nuance. Humans are complex as hell and that nuance should be considered a sacred context. We need to be looking at the specificity of the patient's personal experience. Reducing healing to black and white billing rules results in overdiagnosis, overmedication, and oversimplification. I saw it happen constantly.

The scary part is, the system rewards this behavior. Insurance companies want proof that "treatment is necessary." So well-intentioned doctors who want to get their patients treatment learn how to play the game. They learn how to document that someone has failed multiple antidepressants to get their patient access to something stronger like transcranial magnetic stimulation (TMS) or be eligible for intranasal ketamine. Psychiatrists learn how to pile on the diagnoses that justify the drugs, learning to bend the truth to help their patients, because that's what the system requires. But by doing so these same doctors, who want to help, are silently upholding a system that's deeply flawed.

It's not their fault, at least not most of them. These doctors have hundreds and thousands in student loan debt to repay and cannot up and leave at the next frustration or injustice they witness. I once worked with a senior during a shift in the psych ER. She told me, while holding her forehead (stressed AF), if she were to leave she might contemplate suicide because there is no other way to pay off her debt.

In Western psychiatry, the priority is speed: get the diagnosis, get the drug, move on. If the first medication doesn't work, slap on a new label, prescribe a different pill, and manage the side effects with even more medication.

What gets lost in all this speed is depth. There is no time to ask *why* it is the patient is hurting. No space to hold grief. No curiosity about trauma that didn't start with the patient, but is rooted to their mother, grandmother, or someone who's been dead for decades. It becomes a cycle of symptom management, not actual deep healing.

WHY WE HAVE TO LOOK AT THE SYSTEM

It's easy to point fingers at individual psychiatrists and say they're doing it wrong. But that's not the full truth. The problem isn't one bad doctor here or a careless therapist there (although, truth be told, psychiatrists tend to have some of the biggest unintegrated shadows), it's the entire system that's built to function in a way that lacks soul.

Interestingly, psyche in Latin means soul. Psyche-atry. So tell me, where is the soul?

During my residency I saw this firsthand. I had mentors who genuinely cared. Program directors who were maternal, thoughtful, and did everything they could do. But they were still stuck inside a system that couldn't support the kind of healing they wanted to provide. There were rules, protocols, codes of conduct, and strict guidelines they had to follow to keep their licenses.

You can't break the rules when the rules are the foundation of your job. That's why the downsides of Western psychiatry are not just an individual blame game. It's a system-level problem.

I've attended two different spiritual women's retreats—one in France and the other in Peru—where I met young women who told me about the nightmares of being admitted to psychiatric wards. One shared that she had been molested and raped in a so-called "psychiatric care facility." Outrageous. She went on to describe how the doctor would barely spend five minutes with her, asking only if she still had suicidal thoughts. By the end, she and others had learned to game the system, denying such thoughts just to escape the mental prison as quickly as possible.

Psychiatry in the Western world is deeply entangled with insurance companies, pharmaceutical incentives, and institutional red tape. Hospitals rely on reimbursements to function, which means treatment plans have to look a certain way on paper. And that's exactly what the DSM was created for—to code, categorize, and comply. Psychiatrists spend more time in front of the damn computer typing notes versus actual time spent in human interaction with their patients. I have a lot of genuine empathy for my colleagues in Western medicine, they are doing the best they can, and student loan debts keep them stuck and handcuffed.

So I'm not over here saying we need to throw out the entire psychiatric profession or demonize practitioners. But we do need to tell the truth about the structure we're working within. When we have good intentions, if we don't question the system, we end up reinforcing it.

Western psychiatry isn't all bad. It saves lives. It saved my mom's life and my own at certain points. Bless Zoloft and Klonopin. But it was never meant to do everything. It's one piece of a much larger puzzle. And the more we cling to it as the only valid framework for healing, the more we stay stuck in a narrow paradigm.

OPENING PANDORA'S BOX

Growing up, there was never any question that I would become a doctor. It was pretty much ingrained in me since age 10. My upbringing was very Western-medicine focused, so it wasn't until well into my adulthood that I ever started exploring alternative healing options.

But as I entered my residency and began to see all the flaws in the Western medical system, that crack in Pandora's box began to widen. I wish someone told me sooner that it meant spending almost 9-10 hours in front of a computer screen in a 12-hour shift at the ER. I wanted to help people, and I wanted to do it better than how I'd been taught. That eagerness to see what other healing options were out there led me to start uncovering new options layer by layer. I started to dip my toes in holistic healing modalities.

It started on a trip to Mexico. I was in Tulum, staying at this beautiful place with one of my girlfriends. I remember walking up to the front desk and seeing that the spa menu listed Reiki as one of the offerings. I got so excited. You can get a massage anywhere in the world, but it's rare to find Reiki as part of a spa service. And since I'd never done Reiki before, I wanted to try it out. I'm a curious cat like that.

But the woman at the front desk told me they were fully booked. I was flying out before the next available appointment. I must've looked visibly disappointed because then she said, "Okay, the hotel doesn't have Reiki available right now, but I have a very close friend who is a Reiki master. Her name is Andy. She could come after hours and offer the session in your room."

And I was like, "Absolutely, yes!"

That night, Andy came to my room and gave me my very first Reiki session. And though I didn't know it at the time, that moment marked the beginning of my spiritual awakening.

During the session, I was still very much in my "doctor brain." I had my rational, clinical hat on, thinking, *Okay...she's just moving her hands over me. What is this?* I kept trying to intellectualize it. My left brain was working overtime asking, *How is this working? Is this doing anything?*

And then suddenly, I started feeling actual physical sensations. I felt this tingling and it felt as if I could *feel* the energy moving through my body.

After the session, I felt amazing. I could literally feel my chakras opening. It was like something had been unlocked inside of me. Reiki was an energetic key that opened a door I didn't even know was there.

Reiki was the gateway. I know how that sounds coming from a doctor, and yet that was my truth, and it surprised me too. When I went home, I started booking sessions regularly. It was actually Andy who first suggested to me Family Constellation. After I told her about my past, she kept nudging me, saying, "You need to look into FC. You need to try this." And that's how it works—once you say yes to healing, the path starts revealing itself. One person leads you to the next, and they lead you to the next. Each one shows up at exactly the right time, like feathers dropped from the universe.

THE FALSE BINARY

When I booked my first Reiki session, I didn't know I was opening a door I wouldn't be able to close. Once you are awake you cannot go back to sleep. But as I began exploring alternative forms of healing, I began to see how limited our understanding of healing and energy really is when we view it only through the lens of Western medicine.

One of the biggest problems with Western psychiatry is that it treats itself like the only truth. It reduces everything to neurotransmitters, diagnoses, and medications. Western medicine follows the rule that you have to see it to believe it. If it can't be measured and replicated, it can't be real.

Flip the coin, and you find a different path to healing. On the holistic side, you find practices and traditions known as Eastern medicine, holistic healing, witchy rituals, and so on. Basically, anything that operates in the unseen. This side of healing recognizes energy and honors natural cycles. It works with the elements, aligns with spirit, and uses the body as a compass. This form of healing isn't always logical or linear. Instead it's intuitive and deep, and it's freaking powerful.

Like the yin and yang, both sides are essential. I compare Western and Eastern medicine as the difference between masculine and feminine energy. Western medicine is masculine; it's structured, logical, fast, and focused on doing. It wants results, outcomes, and data. It demands certainty. On the other side, you have the Earth-based approaches like Eastern and holistic traditions; these are feminine. They're receptive, intuitive, slow, and cyclical. They ask you to listen rather than fix. They honor complexity, emotion, and the spaces in between, inviting you to trust your body's innate and unique wisdom.

It's not that one is better than the other. The problem is when we treat them like opposites that can't coexist. When we say,

"You're either science or spirit. Doctor or healer. Rational or intuitive." That's where we go wrong.

Real healing lives in the integration of the two. A big nugget of wisdom I learned from my therapist is "It's *and* not *or*, Meher." I am going to say that one more time because we all are guilty of swinging the pendulum from one extreme to another: Life is *and* not *or*.

I didn't leave psychiatry because I stopped believing in medicine. I left because I couldn't keep pretending that medicine alone was enough. You don't need to pick sides. I still believe in the power of Western tools. If someone is suicidal or in acute distress, then yes, absolutely, go to the hospital. Get the medication. Stabilize your nervous system. Western medicine has a place. It exists for a reason.

I want to be clear: I'm not anti-medication. Medication can be lifesaving. I've seen it bring someone back from the edge of suicide. I've seen it stabilize someone long enough for them to start making new choices, to feel safe in their own body again. There are moments when the nervous system is so dysregulated that the body literally can't access healing tools without first being stabilized.

The problem isn't the medication. The problem is when medication is the only thing on the table. When it's handed out like a solution instead of being used as a bridge.

It's all about discernment. You'll hear me use that word *a lot* in this book because discernment is the most important thing. You need to be able to judge well, to look inside yourself and hear what your body is telling you, to determine when medication is essential or when it's being used as a crutch.

Healing doesn't live in neat boxes. It lives in paradox. In contradiction. We need more room for that in mental health. We need to stop pretending that logic is superior to wisdom or that science has nothing to learn from the soul. If anything, what we call "witchy" and "delulu" today is what ancient cultures called medicine for thousands of years and what many Indigenous cultures still view as sacred, healing medicine. Mental illnesses were celebrated as initiations into psychic gifts by ancient traditions. Shamans and spiritual teachers helped people navigate the complexity that came with these gifts.

Healing requires both the mind of the masculine and the soul of the feminine. It's time we stop fighting about which one is better and start learning how to hold both.

That's why I fell in love with Family Constellations. It's the perfect alignment of science and spirituality. The language of the soul. The more you try to separate yourself from one side— whether it's your family, your culture, or your training—the more life will humble you. You're not here to reject where you come from. You're here to integrate it. That's the true medicine.

Always come back to discernment. To heal, we must know when to use what. We have to stop pretending these systems are enemies and start asking how we can reduce the separation. Honestly, no one's getting helped when Western psychiatry rolls its eyes at spirituality and calls it woo, and spiritual communities scream that Western doctors are all poisoning people. That back-and-forth doesn't serve anyone. It keeps us stuck.

You can't throw the baby out with the bucket.[9]

EARTH MEDICINE AND MENTAL HEALTH

You can't intellectualize your way into healing. I know. It's rude.

You have to feel it. Move through it. Let it live in your body before it can leave your body. That's what Earth medicine taught me.

I think we forget that healing doesn't only happen in therapy rooms or hospitals. It happens in forests. In oceans. In moonlight. In grief rituals and full-body sobs. It happens when your bare feet touch the earth. When you drink water like it's holy. When you cry on the bathroom floor and ask the Universe to hold you.

Western psychiatry taught me to look at mental health through a biochemical lens. Through that lens, I see the imbalances, diagnoses, and medication. And sometimes that lens is helpful. But it's also incomplete. In a system that has swung too much to the side of masculine or the patriarchy, how do we bring it back more into equilibrium, especially for women. For me, the answer is by incorporating Earth medicine. Earth has her own way of understanding what we call depression, anxiety, grief,

---

9 Funny side note: I had no idea what this idiom meant until my mentor, Dr. Schwartz was teaching me about antipsychotics used in the 1970s and used this in a sentence, "...baby with the bucket." What does that mean? He then took out his notepad that he carried with him everywhere and started drawing a baby and a bucket to explain the meaning behind this profound sentence. It was so cute.

or dissociation. Mother Gaia loves us all unconditionally and provides everything to sustain our lives.

In Earth medicine, emotions aren't disorders, they're messengers. Rage is sacred, grief is your capacity to love, and fear is trying to keep you safe. All emotions are meant to be noticed, to be heard. Depression is seen as descent, a call inward, a time to rest and compost (it means you need DEEP REST).

That's why I now try to track my life by the seasons. Winter is a time to rest, spring is for waking up, while summer is for action. In the fall, you start to slow down again as you reap the rewards of the hard work you planted. Nature doesn't bloom year-round and neither should we. Trust me it's hard to follow and sustain a cyclical life in a 3D material world. Women's jobs, for example, are not in alignment with their moon cycle, which affects their productivity on a week by week basis. Our best effort can make a significant difference.

When I left residency, I didn't just leave a job; I also left an identity. I left the linear, hyperproductive, keep-climbing ladder that Western medicine had taught me to chase. And in that void, the Earth welcomed me back to myself. I started noticing the moon cycles. I started spending time in water, not just bathing, but praying in water. Like, literally bowing my head and going into deep prayer while in the bathtub. I have noticed a shift for myself by honoring the element of water, having deep gratitude for holding space for me on my toughest days. It's like being back in the primordial womb. This has definitely improved the relationship with my own inner waters, my emotions.

There's something about connecting with Earth's cycles that brings you home to your body. Despite what your trauma is, if you spend enough time in nature, barefoot, without your phone, with the sun on your face, something in you softens. Something in you remembers who you used to be. Who you are under the roles and systems you grew up in. You remember what it feels like to belong to the Earth, not just live on it. You remember the sacredness of your body and its connection to nature and that you're not separate from the Earth, but made of it.

And I'm not saying that herbs and moon rituals are going to heal every mental health issue. Again, healing is about balance and discernment. Western medicine exists for a reason and it should be used appropriately. What I am saying is that we *are* nature. And when we forget that, we suffer.

If your nervous system is fried, go sit under a tree, take off your shoes, and dig your toes into the dirt. When you walk barefoot on the earth, you absorb her negative ions, which then enter your bloodstream and create biochemical reactions, boosting your serotonin, the happy hormone. In Japan, practitioners prescribe forest bathing for mental health struggles. In Iceland, they prescribe bathing in the mineral rich Blue Lagoon for skin disorders like eczema. These are the teachings that don't come with a prescription. They come from the land. From your lineage. From a time before everything was clinical and commodified.

Ask yourself how you can live in better harmony with the cycles of Mother Nature. How can you live more sustainably? And more broadly, in what ways can we as humans stop poisoning

Earth, which provides us all these resources and elements? How do we live in harmony with nature and not take, take, take, take, take?

Improving your personal relationship with individual elements, you can watch life transform and find your own unique version of wholeness. Honor water, honor your emotions. And it can work alongside your meds, your therapy, and your modern coping tools. We don't need to replace one system with another. We need to remember that healing is older than any system.

ANCIENT ANCESTRAL WISDOM

Our ancestors didn't heal in hospitals. They healed in the dirt, in ceremony with their community using ritual, rhythm, plants, and prayers as their medicine. They tracked the moon, followed the sun, and listened to the land. They fell asleep at dusk and woke up at dawn. They knew that the body and the Earth are not separate.

And while they may not have had the scientific language we use today, and they didn't use the DSM or any diagnostic codes, they had wisdom we've forgotten. They knew how to grieve together. How to lay a body down in the forest and let Earth take what could no longer be carried.

That's why I believe so deeply in ancestral healing. When I started doing this work, I realized I wasn't only healing for myself. I was healing for my mother, for her mother, and for the women who came before them—many of whom never had the choice to do this work in their lifetime. It is because of our ancestors' sacrifices we are here alive and breathing today.

You're reading this book because your soul chose to heal for all the generations that came before you. You're a generational curse-breaker, baby. So as you're doing this work, here's a trippy thing to wrap your mind around: Shadows are not only dark, they're also luminous.

Ancestral healing doesn't only mean looking at what was traumatic. It also means remembering what was powerful, sacred, and gifted, that which eventually became buried under silence, shame, or survival. My best friend's mother, who passed away a few years ago, gifted her with an amazing voice. A voice so resonant, so beautiful that it will ripple through the collective in ways her mother could never have imagined. This is how ancestral gifts live on through our voices, our art, our medicine, our presence. When we heal, we make space for the gifts our ancestors gave to us to finally come alive. My own dear mother had a floral register that she used to write in. She was writing a book and wanted to title it *Flower Power* but never got the chance to finish it. That breaks my heart, and it's one of the catalysts for me completing this book.

We often talk about shadow in terms of pain. Shadow work means facing our shame, rage, or our hidden wounds. But the shadow isn't always dark. Sometimes it's bright. Sometimes, it's the power you see in someone else and don't recognize in yourself. That's called the luminous shadow.

The luminous shadow can be the healer you admire. The writer who makes you feel something. The woman whose presence makes you whisper to yourself in admiration of her charisma, *I could never be like that…*

When you hold deep admiration for someone else, it's because there is a part of your soul you haven't yet owned. You are seeing your own potential. Untapped shadow gold. Just like we inherit pain, we also inherit power we haven't claimed.

I see this all the time in healing spaces. People worship their teachers. They turn their mentors into gods. Spiritual guru culture runs rampant because people are projecting their inner power outward. We say things like, "She's so powerful" or "He's so tapped in," forgetting that the only reason we can even recognize that power is *already alive in us.*

We're not meant to idolize our guides. We're meant to remember that we *are* the altar. And when we forget that, we give our power away. We let someone else be the authority. We wait for their approval instead of trusting our own body. STOP giving your power away!

That's why Family Constellations changed my life. It says yes, trauma lives in your body and nervous system *and* on a soul level. It says you don't have to pick between neuroscience and ancestral wisdom. You can believe in epigenetics and still buy your great-grandmother flowers in spiritual reverence.

In Family Constellations, I learned that healing happens when you stop rejecting where you come from. When you stop pretending you're above your lineage and start seeing that the same blood runs through your veins. Everybody has the right to belong. As you read this book, I invite you to consider, what are some of the ancestral gifts that run in your lineage? Which of these may you have inherited and can tap further into?

You don't break generational cycles by abandoning your roots. You do it by looking back, unburdening the patterns that no longer serve your evolution, while also reclaiming the heirlooms of wisdom that were always yours to keep. I am deeply grateful for the courage that runs through my veins, woven into my Punjabi lineage, and for my grandmother's exquisite taste, her knack for finding the best quality in everything. It's in our blood to rise, to evolve, and to heal. And as we step forward, our nervous systems become the alchemy where all the healing begins.

CHAPTER 4

IT'S NOT YOU, IT'S YOUR NERVOUS SYSTEM

Wholeness is not achieved by cutting off a portion of one's being, but by integration of the contraries.
–CARL JUNG

We've all seen the wellness spiral. Maybe you've been in one and felt the midnight urge to fix every part of your life overnight. You feel anxious, exhausted, or vaguely unwell, and before you know it, you're six internet tabs deep into meditation playlists, full moon rituals, and trauma healing reels. Everyone says if you're feeling yucky just meditate. Journal about it. Banish those thoughts and raise your vibration, babe.

I myself still struggle with this. I have five different tabs open in my mind's browser for all the creative projects I am birthing. It is ungrounding. I do not see this tendency improving overnight. However, I used to have ten tabs open. And if in the next six months, I can cut down from five tabs to three, that's still progress in my personal healing journey. I'm still making headway in shedding the unhelpful archetype of overachiever. I'm trying to hold compassion for this perfectionist part of myself. Don't get me wrong, ambition is a beautiful thing; it's what fuels us. It's the creative fire element, that spark of motivation. But fire can also burn you, deplete you, and leave you exhausted.

So what if you're trying all the "right" tools and still feel like shit? What if every morning you light your sage, form your hand mudras, and focus on your breathing, but your mind still won't shut the hell up? Instead, the voices in your head are just getting louder.

Your Instagram stories tell everyone you're in your healing era, but no matter how much you sit in silence or write novels in your journal, the wounds from your past won't close up.

All these wellness influencers telling people to heal through meditation alone are promoting a superficial way of healing. It's surface level. It doesn't go deep enough to reach the root of the trauma. Do this thing and you'll feel better. Think positive. Light a candle. Ignore the bad thoughts until they go away. It's all rooted in a kind of hopeful ignorance. It's spiritual bypassing 101 and I'm sometimes guilty of it too. I mean, it's not fun actually sitting with the comfort of grief or shame when you can gaslight yourself into feeling "higher vibe" emotions or listening to affirmations to reprogram your subconscious.

"Meditate your way out of everything" is mainstream wellness advice, but that doesn't mean it works. Alchemy requires listening to the innate wisdom of your body, sitting with those shitty feelings we all naturally tend to avoid like the plague. A lot of sources say that your body is your unconscious mind.[10] As someone looking for healing, using meditation as your one and only tool is an innocent mistake because it's often made without a deep understanding of trauma, nervous system regulation, or somatic safety. You're dipping your toe into the healing process. It feels productive and spiritual, like you're doing something. But it can actually make things worse.

Again, I love meditating, so don't misinterpret this as me being anti-meditation. Remember we don't throw the baby out with the bucket.

As with Western medicine, there is a time, a place, and purpose for everything. I'm not telling you not to meditate or journal. What I am saying is meditation alone will not heal your trauma. And meditation may not be the right tool to use at the beginning of your healing journey, not when you've just opened up your Pandora's box of trauma.

SAFETY IS YOUR BESTIE

It doesn't matter how often you're meditating—you could be meditating five times a day and it won't make much of a difference—if you're stuck in a trauma-triggering environment. Environmental safety is foundational.

10 Charles Martin, "Ego, Self, Body and the Unconscious," Dr. Charles Martin Therapy, accessed August 13, 2025, https://drcharlesmartin.com/ego-self-body-the-unconscious/#:~:text=The%20body%20is%20often%20seen,and%20thus%20to%20becoming%20whole.

Let me make something clear: You cannot heal in the same environment that made you sick.

You've probably heard of the fight-or-flight response, but what doesn't get talked about enough is the freeze response. Freeze is your body's way of saying, "I can't run. I can't fight. So I'll shut down to survive." It's a primal response to fear as your nervous system is doing whatever it can to keep you alive. Our body goes lengths to endure the unconscious self-sabotage behaviors we all struggle with.

Think of a deer being hunted by a predator. Once the deer realizes it can't escape, it goes completely still. On the outside, it looks calm. But inside, its body is in overdrive. It's hyperaware of the threat, but also preparing for death. To the limbic system, freezing is one level above death. It serves as a function for safety as the body is preparing to die. Physiologically, the breath slows down, the heart starts pumping and redistributing blood to the vital organs for survival.

When the deer is frozen, both its sympathetic and parasympathetic nervous systems are activated. The sympathetic system prepares the body for action—think fight-or-flight—while the parasympathetic system is responsible for rest, recovery, and calming the body. When both systems turn on at the same time, it creates an internal paralysis.

Now, think of an opossum, or another kind of animal that plays dead when threatened. When an animal plays dead, its body gives off all the correct hormonal signals so the predator cannot sniff the prey properly. It can't gauge that the prey is actually alive, so it might leave the prey alone in search of something fresher. Suppose the animal is unlucky and the predator takes the prey anyway. In that case, the freeze response can potentially make death less painful by numbing pain and reducing the intensity of the trauma.

That's in the wild and it obviously doesn't apply to those of us who live in the modern world and don't deal with predators hunting us for their evening meal. And yet the same shutdown happens in humans who've endured chronic fear, emotional neglect, or unsafe environments for too long. For example, humans who have experienced sexual abuse may freeze like a deer in headlights when they see someone who reminds them of their abuser. It's a safety mechanism to cope. Our bodies are always trying to protect us.

And often, we don't even realize it's happening. As a human species, evolution has made our lives easier. However, our body, which is represented by the slow moving earth element, cannot keep up with the mind's rapid evolution. The mind, represented by the element of air, is the fastest moving element.

There is a famous saying, "Where wisdom reigns, there is no conflict between thinking and feeling." That level of wisdom can take years to achieve. Trauma healing is more undoing and unlearning than doing more.

It is funny that the hardest thing for humanity today is to slow down. To use my own example, in therapy they tell the therapists not to give advice. The only advice my therapist actually ever offered to me was when she asked me to set a timer for five minutes and do nothing. Not even meditate. It's hysterical and pathetic at the same time that the hardest task for me is to do absolutely nothing. Doing is how I coped in my childhood. I used multitasking as a constant distraction to avoid my pain, my grief, and the pain of my mother's illness.

In the human world, signs that you're in a freeze response might look like distracting yourself like I did. You might experience dissociation or feeling disconnected from your body. It could also look like:

- Chronic procrastination
- Feeling emotionally numb
- Knowing what to do but not being able to do it; feeling stuck
- Overintellectualizing your healing, saying, "I think I know why I feel like this," without embodying the experience
- A life that looks fine on the outside but feels flat on the inside

It's that inability to take action, feeling a sense of hopelessness and doom. It's like, you know you can do better, but because your need for safety is so exhausted, it's hard to do anything about it.

You can't think your way out of a freeze state. You also can't meditate, journal, or "raise your vibration" out of it, if your body still feels like it's in danger.

Freezing is not a mindset issue. You're not stuck in chronic procrastination because you are lazy. Energy at this point is depleted for you. You're stuck there for survival. And no matter how much Instagram or TikTok scrolling you do, you won't be able to get out of that state until the body starts thawing. And the best way to turn on defrost mode is to make the conscious decision to heal the shit that fucked you up in the first place.

The first thing you need to do when you're ready to open Pandora's box of trauma and start healing it, is to find yourself a safe environment. That means your own space where your nervous system can exhale. It can't be the same place that you grew up, if that's where the source of trauma is coming from. At least, not for a certain amount of time. Not until you've been away, healed the trauma, and feel safe enough to return. It sucks, but it's true.

That's why my healing journey really started when I came to the United States at 27. My family thinks I've "Americanized" since moving, but the truth is I had to be by myself for a while so I could actually discover who I am outside of my tribe. I miss them dearly, and yet I choose to live my own version of life. It is a juggling act between belonging and not self-betraying in the process.

Beyond that, I couldn't truly start healing while I was still working in psychiatry at the hospital. I was constantly in a state of hypervigilance. I remember waking up in the morning and the first thing I'd do was open my inbox, completely petrified. *Who did I piss off? What mistake did I make? What charting error is waiting for me? Do I have an email from a "higher up" scolding me about something?* As I now see it retrospectively, I wore a fake mask of inauthenticity to blend in.

So after your home environment, the next thing you need to look at is your job. In the world we live in, so much of your life gets funneled into where you sleep and where you work. Both need to feel safe. When you wake up in the morning, what do you do? You go to work. If that space isn't safe, your nervous system won't feel safe either.

I hate to break it to you, but this is part of the healing journey. It's like the Tower card in Tarot—everything that was built on a false foundation has to crumble. And the more you cling to your old identity, the more it hurts. It's like holding on to a rope that's cutting into your hand and soul. It will bleed and hurt more the longer you hold on. Eventually, you have to let go.

The months leading up to my decision to actually quit were excruciating. I was stuck in the in-between of should I stay and complete the final two years or should I dump almost 12 years of hard work that I had invested into this profession?

LET IT BURN DOWN

When you decide to let go, when you decide to choose your safety over the things that have caused trauma, chaos will erupt. So when things start falling apart, let them fall. The cycle of transformation requires death and rebirth.

Now listen, it's easy to sit here and say that once you're over the hump. But when you're in it? When everything is crumbling? It's terrifying. I don't want to tell you that it's not. A big reason why I wrote this book is because I want to validate your fear. This shit is scary. The unknown is scary. When your life starts unraveling, it's not pretty or poetic. It's terrifying AF.

So instead of telling you what you should do in those moments, I just want to say: I see you. And it's okay to be afraid. It is really scary.

No matter how many times someone gives you advice or external validation like when your spiritual mentors or therapists or friends say things like, "The bigger the leap, the bigger the quantum shift in your reality." It still feels so uncertain. You might know, intellectually, that what they're saying is true. But that doesn't make it feel less terrifying when you are in the vortex.

I remember panicking about it to close friends after I left my residency. I was freaked out. I didn't know what I was going to do with my career. I was 30 years old and starting over. Every morning I'd wake up with anxiety filling up my chest as I'd remember, my heart palpating, and needing to pop an SOS (take as needed) prescription Klonopin: *Oh, my god! I quit residency. What have I done?*

I remember talking to one of my best friends, Bobby, and expressing how stressed out I was. And in response he looked at me grinning and said, "I'm so excited for you. I'm so excited. This is amazing." I felt like punching him.

Like, my goodness. I feel like I'm literally dying right now. My life is falling apart. How can you be smiling at me?!

I remember crying to his wife, sobbing and saying, "I'm dying out here. I'm crying. I'm submerged in shame and guilt and fear." And he was standing next to us, grinning like some enlightened maniac.

His response was, "This is amazing. You're moving through it so fast. I'm so excited for you."

And I'm like, "I hate you."

There are so many people who will tell you, "It's so much brighter on the other side."

And it fucking better be.

Because once you choose to move forward, there is no going back.

When I left psychiatry, I fully cut the cord. My program director even called me the day I quit and said, "Meher, do you want to stay for one more month? That way, we can give you a certificate that you completed two full years of residency."

It would have been good to have, just in case I ever wanted to come back to Western medicine. And logically, it made perfect sense. I was two weeks away from starting my third year. One more month and I'd have a safety net. If I ever changed my mind, I could come back and finish the last two years. It would have been the "smart" choice.

But I said no. I tuned into my heart. Isn't that what real bravery is? To feel fear but to still do it anyways? Bravery is not the absence of fear but rather still moving forward despite it.

Enough. That marked the moment I chose myself.

All I kept telling myself was, *This is my choice. This is my decision. Do not let your mind fear you. I will not listen to my mind.* I kept repeating it like a mantra: *I'm not listening to my mind. I'm not listening to my mind.*

Because my mind wanted to make it softer. It wanted me to be more logical, make the safe choice, create the safety net. *Maybe just one more month, Meher. Maybe take the certificate. Maybe ease out instead of cutting the cord.*

But I had listened to my mind my entire life. It was time to listen to my heart for once.

Leaving residency was the first decision I ever made purely from the heart. And it took courage—real, heart-led courage. I am so proud of how brave I am. The word "courage" comes from the French *corage*, which traces back to the Latin *cor*, meaning "heart."[11] Courage means heart. At that moment, I had to trust that following my heart was enough. And when you're standing at the edge of a big leap, I think it's important to remember that.

And yeah, what they say is true: the bigger the jump, the bigger the reality shift. My best friend had a right to be excited for me because he knew that I was on the precipice. But that didn't stop me from wanting to wipe that silly grin off his face, grab him, and scream about how scared I was. Because even though my mind knew he was right and that I was on the edge of something great, my body was frozen with fear. And that fear is valid. So if you're feeling that fear right now, I want you to know that being afraid is normal. You are valid in what you're feeling.

You are valid in feeling that fear, AND it's still helpful to have someone on the sidelines cheering you on. I am so grateful

---

11 "Courage," *Online Etymology Dictionary*, accessed May 27, 2025, https://www.etymonline.com/word/courage.

to the Universe and Bobby for support in that time of utter despair.

My advice is, as you're digging through the shit and facing the fear, keep someone close to you—a trusted friend, mentor, or coach—someone who's been through the dark night of the soul. It doesn't matter what role they play in your life, as long as they're someone who's made it through to the other side. Someone who can look at you and say, "You're not crazy. You're just in the middle. You will not feel like this forever. There is light at the end of the tunnel."

When you're in the dark void, you can't see the light, but the people who've made it through the void can. I had to keep reminding myself of that. When I told Meera how scared I was, and she told me it would be okay, I had to remember that she knew because she'd been through it too. This is a woman who was a single mother, living on food stamps, cut off by her family; and the very next year, she made six figures.

If she can do that, so can I. I can do it in my own way and so can you in your own unique way.

THAWING YOUR BODY

When you're frozen, it feels impossible to move at all. But you can move, and you have to. With that first step, you must make the moves you need to create a safe environment. A safe place to sleep and a safe place to work. And then, what? How do you get rid of the trauma that's plaguing you?

What if you've already tried everything—meditating, journaling, doing the shadow work—and you're still frozen?

It's so easy in those moments to slip into the belief that there's something wrong with you. That you're too far gone. Let me be clear: You are not broken. You are frozen. And you've been trying to heal in a world that doesn't understand trauma to its fullest depths.

If meditation hasn't worked for you, it's not because you're doing it wrong. It's probably because your nervous system wasn't ready for that kind of stillness. For people with trauma, meditation can trap you further in your thoughts, amplify your inner critic, or push you deeper into dissociation. For people carrying complex PTSD or deep layers of shame, meditation can actually make things worse, not better. The inner critic gets louder, and the shame gets sharper. You sit down to find peace, and instead, you're flooded with self-judgment.

Sometimes what you need, more than silence, is to get back into your body.

That's why early in my healing, I turned to somatic work: body scans, reiki energy healing, grounding, breath work, somatic yoga, walks, acupuncture, and movement. These movements helped me feel my limbs again and helped me come back into my skin. You don't need a ten-step morning routine. You need your breath and to feel your feet on the floor so you can ground into this earthly reality and dimension. It may sound paradoxical but in nervous system healing and mastery, the slower the better.

So many of us are trying to heal from the neck up. We're making decisions with our heads, disconnected from the deep yes or no that lives in our bodies. When you've been hurt or unsafe, your body becomes the last place you want to live. So you hover above it and intellectualize your healing instead of embodying it. That's why, for some people, meditation only deepens the dissociation. It reinforces the mental loop, forcing you to relive the trauma in your mind without giving your body the chance to safely process it.

To truly live a full life you have to let your soul be seated in your earthly vessel: your miraculous body. We have been put on this planet for a reason, to enjoy earthly pleasures and to not spiritually bypass them. Ascension and raising your vibration are the end goals but "tapping into higher dimensions," "connecting to source," and all of those spiritual taglines should not come at the cost of escaping your material reality and the matrix. In my humble opinion, I think that's what psychosis is: having an open third-eye chakra without a grounded root chakra, leaving you unsteady in this earthly reality. This is why in psychosis you cannot distinguish what is real and what is not.

If you're just starting your healing journey, I'd much rather you do something that brings you gently back into your body instead of locking you deeper into your head. That's why I recommend somatic work. Go to YouTube and search for somatic exercises. Start with something simple: a body scan, a grounding breath, even lying on the floor and noticing your weight. Let your body lead. Everything is available for free on YouTube, and you can find everything from breathwork to chanting to somatic yoga and stretches. You don't need me to add one more to-do on your healing journey agenda and give you a grocery list of rituals and exercises to perform. Trust your inner wisdom.

MANIFESTATION

So you know how everyone is into manifestation these days, right? Let me give it to you straight with some hardcore truths about this topic. What's the point of healing, unburdening from trauma, and breaking free from generational patterns if you can't actually enjoy your life or step into the role of consciously creating your reality? Manifesting the dreams and visions of your heart, especially around abundance, is part of why we do this work.

First things first: One of the biggest blocks to your material desires is karmic debt from past lives and unconscious loyalty to your ancestors and their struggles, suffering, and fate. Later in this book, we'll dive into the therapeutic work of Systemic and Family Constellations as a way to release these karmic loops and familial entanglements.

But for now, and more importantly for the purpose of this chapter on your nervous system, I want to clarify something: You can absolutely manifest your dream life with a dysregulated, even fried, nervous system. The line between your dreams coming true and the fear your nervous system holds is razor thin. Manifestation isn't about chasing a constant calm, Zen-like state. It's about expanding your body's capacity to tolerate the dysregulation that comes when life actually meets your desires.

Here's a vulnerable example: I just moved into my dream home in LA right by the Pacific Ocean. Part of me feels so alive and grateful, and another part of me is terrified because my dreams are literally coming true. That's why they say, "Be careful what you wish for—you just might get it."

As I was nearing the end of this manuscript, I noticed myself slipping back into self-sabotaging behaviors: smoking more weed after a long sober stretch, reaching for my SOS prescription Klonopin more often. My shadow was pulling hard, fear was lodged in my chest and belly, trying to keep me "safe" from stepping into too much power, too much visibility, too much expansion.

I share this with you because I'm human and flawed, like everyone else. I don't have my shit together all the time, even after years of deep healing work. Healers need healers. There's no shame in seeking extra support when life is stretching you beyond what feels comfortable.

POWER OF DISCERNMENT

Now, let me say this too: You don't need to do everything all at once. In the age of Instagram spirituality, it's easy to get overwhelmed by the pressure to do more breathwork, Reiki, sound baths, cacao ceremonies, biohacking, ancestral healing, quantum leaping, inner child work, nervous system rewiring, and so on. It's all beautiful and valid and it all has its time and place.

But you are not meant to consume it all at once like some spiritual all-you-can-eat buffet. Doing that will deep fry your already short circuiting nervous system. I'd much rather see you delete social media, forget all the tips and tricks for a while, silence the outside noise, and come back home to your own self.

Trauma is a biological, ancestral, and environmental survival adaptation. It isn't healed by gorging on self-improvement trends. That's why discernment is so important. When you come across a new modality, ask yourself: *Can I actually integrate this right now? Do I have the energy to learn this and apply it? Or am I doing it because I feel like I should? Does my mind say **yes** like an excited child while my body says **no** like a wise inner parent?*

And if your intuition tells you no, remember no now doesn't mean no forever. Sometimes healing means choosing not to take in more until you're ready. It means decluttering your spiritual to-do list. You may even want to declutter your physical space. Get rid of items in your home, closet, decrease your work load, and see how much more energy you have. I personally can see how light and clean my home feels after getting rid of excess furniture and clothing. It's a spiritual detox and a physical energy cleanse.

I remember my mentor Dr. Schwartz gifted me a psychotherapeutic technique book by Sheldon B. Kopp called, *If You Meet the Buddha on the Road, Kill Him.* Although truth be told, I never got around to reading the book; but the title has stuck with me.

It basically highlights a Zen Buddhism philosophy implying you should not cling to or idolize any teacher, even the Buddha or anyone else in your life pretending to know what is best for you. It emphasizes that true enlightenment comes from within and through one's own experience, not through blind adherence to external figures or teachings. It encourages practitioners to question, doubt, and ultimately transcend even the most revered figures and concepts in their spiritual journey. This is how the foundation of true sovereignty is built.

When your nervous system is ready, when you have the safety, support, and space, you will go deeper. One of my closest mentors, Mia Magik, wrote a book about connecting deeper with our inner wisdom called *IntuWitchin: Learn to Speak the Language of the Universe and Reclaim Your Inner Magik* and I highly recommend it for anyone who is ready for that next step. When you are ready to go deeper, to try new tools, exercises, and rituals, you will know. Let your *IntuWitchin* guide you.

CHAPTER 5

GASLIGHTING YOURSELF

It is an excellent exercise to be entirely honest with oneself.
–SIGMUND FREUD

A few months before I quit residency, I called my dad and told him how miserable I was. I told him how much I hated being a doctor, how I hated going to the hospital, and finally revealed everything I'd been holding back about my career for so long. I straight up told him in a very vulnerable way—not blaming him at all—I said, "You know, Papa, I only became a doctor so that my one available parent would love me."

Stunned, my father said, "I don't remember telling you I wouldn't love you if you were not a doctor. If you ever felt that way, it was a failure on my part as a father. If you hate it so much, leave."

His words were the key to my shackles. I had taken the chance to share with him how I honestly felt, and in return, his words empowered me to realize that nobody else is holding me captive to my own choices. What I would do next was my decision. I could stay in residency and continue being resentful, continue blaming my father for pressuring me into becoming a doctor, or I could decide to do something to support my happiness. My father's words gave me the green light, a free pass. He was telling me that I was free to follow the course of my own liking.

Before that conversation, I used to walk around proud with my resentment trophy. If there were a pageant for Who Can Sacrifice the Most and Still Smile Through It, I would've taken the crown… And cried during the acceptance speech. I used to martyr myself like, I'm doing this for YOU, you know. I'm sacrificing my own happiness for your expectations. But that conversation forced me to take accountability for my actions. From then on, if I chose to stay, it was on me, not anybody else.

My resentment towards family was a shield protecting me from having to make a choice. Yes, I hated my job, but to leave residency and start a new career from scratch at age 30 would be fucking terrifying. It was serving me to tell myself that I've already slogged it out for 12 years, I might as well stay, because that's what my father wants me to do. I represented the stereotypical Indian kid in many ways, with a career path forged in childhood itself to pick between being a doctor, lawyer, or engineer. A stable profession that provides security and earned respect in society.

I learned that true healing requires radical self-honesty. You have to lay all your cards out on the table and face them all. Shadow work is about exploring and integrating the parts of yourself you've repressed or denied. It's about facing the uncomfortable truths beneath your emotions and behaviors and understanding the root of where these feelings come from.

Facing the shadow to find healing in that darkness requires holding yourself accountable, albeit with compassion. When you're honest with yourself, you come out of the victim mindset and begin to embrace a cocreator mode with the Universe. You see the role you've been playing in your own suffering, and you find the empowerment to change the story. It requires you to finally grow up and stop blaming others for your misery.

This chapter is about finding the courage to embody radical self-honesty. Unfiltered honesty is the first step to holding yourself personally accountable. Shadow work is based on the principle of as above, so below, as within, so without. What you do in the microcosm reflects in the macrocosm. Your outer world is a direct reflection of your inner world. If you're telling yourself you are not worthy and come up with excuses to stop yourself from doing what you want to do, that reality will be mirrored back to you. Facing the parts of yourself you project onto others is not flattering, but it's revealing.

I have total and complete compassion for you and what you've been through in your past. Whatever trauma you've faced, whatever happened to you in childhood was not your fault. And I am the first person to tell you that if you want to cry about it, you should cry. You should grieve and mourn what was lost. Let out your pain in whatever way your body needs. But eventually—and this is super important—you need to take accountability for your healing. In the framework of Family Constellations, taking accountability is when you begin the transition from being a child in the system to becoming an adult. Children think someone will come to save them and adults know that only they can save themselves.

VICTIMHOOD VERSUS VICTIM MENTALITY

Before we talk more about why accountability is essential, let's make an important distinction. There's a big difference between being a victim of your circumstances and having a victim mentality. One is situational, the other is an identity. You can absolutely be a victim of trauma, abuse, oppression, or neglect, but if you stay there too long, if you start to internalize that role as who you are, being the victim becomes your comfort zone.

It starts to feel safe to have a victim mentality, especially if you're surrounded by people who validate it. When something is familiar, even if it's painful, it feels less threatening than the unknown.

You might hate the story you're stuck in, but at least you know your lines. Honestly in my case, I had the whole script memorized. My inner monologue deserved an Emmy for Best Performance in a Drama I Secretly Created Myself.

A lot of empaths find themselves stuck in these circumstances. Empaths are people who are highly attuned to the emotions of those around them, often feeling what others feel on a deep level. They sense as if those emotions were their own, and in return, it's natural to want that same external validation.

Empaths want you to see how much they're suffering. They want someone to say, "Look at everything you're carrying. You're so strong. You're so good." Empaths are the Oscar-winning emotional shapeshifters. They'll absorb your sadness, your anger, and still apologize for taking up space. Often they get used to the feeling of victim mentality and stay in toxic situations because they're hoping someone will finally see their pain and offer the love they didn't get the first time they were hurt.

It takes some radical, uncomfortable self-honesty to realize that your victimhood is actually serving you. But that's the essential first step. You must recognize that staying the victim might be protecting you from fear and helping you avoid change. This is how my resentment toward my father was protecting me from facing the unknown.

You need to ask yourself what you truly want from life and what action you are taking to get there. If you're in a relationship, job, or anything else that isn't serving you, ask yourself, what role you're playing in keeping it. Everything has a plus and a minus. Everything serves you in some way. To shed the shadows of your past, you need to name what you've been getting out of it—then decide what you're willing to leave behind.

THE ROLE OF INNOCENCE IN SUFFERING

It's important to recognize the difference between being the victim and holding onto a victim mentality; you must recognize that you always have a choice. I always had a choice in becoming and staying a doctor. But even when we realize we've chosen to stay in the victim mentality, it's important to face that honesty with compassion. We need to remove the shame that keeps us in that position and recognize the innocence that brought us to that space in the first place.

When we finally get honest with ourselves about the choices we've made, the roles we've played, and the ways we've suffered, we uncover pure innocence at the root. The more you realize that, you begin to see that even your most "toxic" patterns were born from innocent, often childlike, desires: the desire to be loved, to belong, to feel safe, to make your parents proud, or to save someone you couldn't save as a child.

I know this from personal experience. My archetype was the wounded healer. This concept comes from Carl Jung and describes someone who, through their own experiences of pain and adversity, gains a profound capacity to heal and empathize with others facing similar challenges. It's no coincidence I became a psychiatrist while growing up with a mother who has schizophrenia. There was an unconscious, superhero-like innocence driving me: *If I can help the world heal, maybe I can save my mother too from her pain.* A lot of people who end up in healthcare or other healing industries carry this wounded healer archetype, and the roots usually go back to our childhood experiences.

For those of us who were parentified children—those who grew up feeling responsible for our parents' emotions or survival—we carry an invisible weight on our shoulders. We believe, often without realizing it, that someone else's fate is in our hands. That if we sacrifice enough, we can fix everything. In Family Constellations we call this the difference between child love and adult love. Child love says, "I'll give up everything to save you." Adult love knows: "I must have boundaries, and I must be able to tolerate guilt that comes from setting those boundaries in order to honor my own life."

Coming to this realization can be humbling. It's a bitter pill to swallow when I suddenly realized, *Who the hell do I think I am that I can save my parents from their fate? And honestly, did they ever actually ask me to?*

But that honesty must be incredibly gentle. If you have trauma—especially trauma tied to perfectionism, people-pleasing, or self-abandonment—then beginning to take accountability can easily activate shame spirals. We're not here for that. Accountability must be rooted in love. You must understand that even the parts of yourself you judge were born from a very young, innocent place that just wanted to be loved.

HURT PEOPLE HURT PEOPLE

A personal example of this comes to mind when I think about my childhood best friend of 20 years. I recently realized that while she was my best friend, I was her bully. It wasn't the obvious kind of bullying, like pushing her down on the schoolyard and taking her lunch money. It was more subtle, a kind of bullying that hides under the guise of care.

Looking back now, with everything I've learned about boundaries and personal safety, I can see how much I used to bulldoze my best friend. I never respected her need for space or freedom. I constantly pushed her to think like me, to agree with me, to adopt my worldview. I remember one moment so clearly when we got into some political debate, and I was hell-bent on making her see it *my* way. At the time, I thought I was being passionate, but now I realize I wasn't respecting her. I was trying to dominate her thoughts under the illusion of righteousness.

I used to show up at her house every day, uninvited, assuming that proximity equaled love. I thought that by bossing her around and pressuring her to think like me, I was showing her love. It was how my family showed me love, as if love is some kind of possession, and love means I know what's best for you. I've always hated it growing up. But it wasn't until recently that I realized I've been guilty too.

Realizing that I was a bully to someone I loved took some radical honesty to admit. No one wants to admit that they've hurt someone they care about. But it also took compassion for me to see my past behavior and not judge myself, to not spiral in a fit of self-hatred or become drenched in the shame of my past actions. I can now recognize that, yes, I was a bully, I can take accountability for the role I played, and use it as a lesson moving forward. But I'm not going to go down a shame spiral for something I did as an ignorant child. And I'm not going to forget that there were two people in that relationship.

I want to be clear: Accountability is not the same as taking 100% responsibility. She had her role too. If someone continues to violate your boundaries and you continue to allow it, both parties are participating in the dynamic. This is similar to an abusive relationship, where one person harms and the other stays. Both people are playing a role, even if that role is shaped by trauma, fear, or survival. In our case, our roles were shaped by our familial conditioning. And just as I have to take accountability for being a bully, my friend now has to face her fate of not being able to put up a stronger boundary, and whatever life lessons were meant for her from that experience. This is not about morality; this is about integrity.

Self-honesty becomes easier when you see the innocence behind your actions. I didn't consciously know it at the time, but looking back now, I can see how trying to control my best friend was my unconscious way of trying to play savior. Because I couldn't save my mother from her illness, I tried to save every other person I met. I thought I knew what was best, and by using force and control, I could, in some covert way, protect the people I cared about. All these acts of boundary violation were committed in the name of innocent love.

Family Constellations defines child love as when you sacrifice every advantage to be like your family with this childlike hope and innocence that your love and your sacrifice will save them. Not everyone grows out of this childlike innocence. Even as adults, if you don't learn how to uphold boundaries and be willing to tolerate the guilt of making different choices from your family, you may remain stuck in that childlike form. You see this in religious violence. In his book *Love's Hidden Symmetry: What Makes Love Work in Relationships*, Bert Hellinger mentions that most acts of violence are committed against others in the name of religion or political morality.

Some of the most severe acts like incest, abuse, and manipulation, are often committed by people who were deeply hurt themselves. Even psychopaths and sociopaths, who we tend to see as irredeemable, usually have tormented childhood stories. People who hurt others have often been profoundly hurt themselves.

This is why I say hurt people hurt people. But it also works the other way too: healed people heal people. We get to choose which category we fall into. When we're honest with ourselves about our past and the roles we've played, we can make sure we fall into the second category. Riding on the high horse of moral superiority keeps us bound to these victim/perpetrator dynamics and stuck in these karmic loops of endless suffering.

SPHERE OF INFLUENCE

Another noteworthy teaching in Constellations is something called the *sphere of influence.* If—and only if—you consciously choose to grow up and step into adulthood through the lens of this work, you should know that men and women move through different spheres.

Men have two spheres of influence. Women have three. I know, literally so rude that we women get an *extra* one to navigate before adulthood, all while learning to tolerate guilt and to face the reality that becoming an adult requires a betrayal of our family system. Choosing guilt means choosing yourself, even if it means no longer remaining blindly loyal to the system you came from.

Frankly, some people choose to remain loyal to their parents for their entire lives. In the field of Constellations, this isn't judged; it's seen as an innocent act of child-love, where a child would willingly sacrifice their own life in order to belong. It is pure.

With that understanding, let's look at the actual path of the spheres.

For men, the sequence is: Mother's sphere → Father's sphere → World/Adulthood

For women, the sequence is: Mother's sphere → Father's sphere → Back to Mother's sphere → World/Adulthood

People can get stuck in a sphere for years, even for life. For example, a man stuck in his mother's sphere often shows narcissistic tendencies, while a woman stuck in her father's sphere displays the same.

According to Hellinger, each sphere can take up to two years to move through, *theoretically.* In practice, who knows how long it actually takes. It depends on the individual and their free will to grow. Personally, I only moved into my father's sphere of influence this year. Loving reminder to myself: progress over perfection.

Which brings me to the next essential piece: guilt. Moving through these spheres isn't possible without learning how to face guilt head-on.

UNDERSTANDING GUILT

If you're going to be radically honest with yourself, you need to know the difference between guilt and shame.

Shame attacks the core of who you are. It makes your very existence feel defective. Whereas guilt points to a behavior, not your identity. It says that you did something wrong (or at least perceived as wrong) per your own values, not that you are inherently wrong for existing. Guilt can be useful because it helps you align with your integrity. You can acknowledge the harm, take responsibility, and course-correct.

I have seen love flourish in joint family systems where people are still thriving. I used to look at that and wonder how it was possible to stay so enmeshed, so connected. I brought it up to Meera once, and she told me how all forms of love must be honored in the field. It is actually considered a pure act of love to betray one's self to stay belonging to one's tribe, despite personal detriment. If someone chooses to stay closely tied to their family of origin—through shared religion, tradition, routine, or unspoken loyalty—that's not something to judge. You must honor everyone's free will.

For me, the stakes were different. My need to individuate felt like life or death. It wasn't optional. I had to break away to survive. When I compare myself to friends who are so close to their family, do I feel guilty for not following that same path? I have before. Does my ego want to put on this air of superiority for being brave enough to break away on my own? It has before.

I needed to break away. Some people don't, and that's okay. Their belonging doesn't make them less evolved, just like my separation doesn't make me any better or worse. You can choose to stay. You can choose to leave. You can choose to carry the guilt of disappointing your family, or not.

Being an adult means having the willingness and capacity to tolerate guilt, however it shows up for you. Once you can build the capacity for tolerating guilt, you can become a sovereign being. You can make choices based solely on your desires and not out of conditioning or people pleasing. You stop making choices to appease your ancestors, stop twisting yourself into knots to avoid disapproval, stop performing loyalty out of fear, and you start choosing from a place of truth. This can be a painful process since often the price of freedom is loneliness.

Not everyone has to follow that path. I don't go back to my hometown and look at my childhood friends who stayed where they grew up, thinking I've evolved and they haven't. Well, maybe just a little bit. I'm only joking. That would be another form of judgment masquerading as insight. Some people are nourished by belonging, while others feel severely triggered by it. Neither experience is wrong. If your circumstances allow you to remain close to your family, and you feel nourished by that, I genuinely say, I love that for you.

Being honest with yourself means being willing to admit which circumstances you truly desire. Are you staying because it's what you want or because it's what someone else wants for you?

In Family Constellations, part of the work requires creating a visual representation of a family system to understand and address patterns and dynamics that might be affecting you. This is called a constellation. I have a cousin who died in a car crash at the age of 21, and because I was feeling immense guilt around his death, I decided to do a self-constellation around it. As I was working on it, I felt like there was some missing puzzle piece that I couldn't put my finger on, until I felt this nudge to bring in my cousin's dad. When I did, the energy shifted completely.

I'd been feeling this massive survivor's guilt so strongly, it was manifesting in my body. My right shoulder was actually lower than my left shoulder because of it, like there was this perpetual weight on my back bringing it down. When I brought my uncle into the constellation, I suddenly realized, the guilt I was carrying wasn't my own, but his. I had been unknowingly carrying guilt on his behalf out of unconscious loyalty. Family

Constellations says we absorb what's unresolved in our lineage as a way to belong. That's the unconscious contract: Let me carry this for you so we can stay connected. When I was able to return the guilt in the constellation, I literally saw my shoulders even out. That's how deeply inherited guilt can root itself into the musculature, the posture, the very structure of your body.

Bert Hellinger called this the difference between primary and secondary feelings. Primary feelings belong to you. You feel them, express them, and they move. Secondary feelings are inherited. They stick around. You feel them intensely, but they're not tied to your life directly. They often show up as emotions that are disproportionate to your circumstances. In my case, it was when I felt waves of inexplicable rage that made no sense until I learned that my great-grandfather was murdered and his body was found decomposing in a water tank. This is what I mean by enmeshment or entanglements in family dynamics, carrying burdens for your ancestors out of loving loyalty.

So when you find yourself stuck and trapped in repeating dynamics and patterns, unable to move forward despite trying after repeated efforts, there may be something deeper to explore with a trauma-informed Family Constellations practitioner. This shit goes beyond the rational mind. The field will show you what needs to be resolved or unburdened. Without that inquiry, you risk remaining stuck or enmeshed with your ancestors' fate for a story that isn't yours to carry. And then you wonder why it never resolves, why the shame doesn't shift, why the guilt won't go away.

LET'S GET RAGEY

Getting honest with yourself, facing the guilt of your past, and basically everything involved in this overall healing journey requires growing up. And let me just say, it's extremely rude that we have to grow up. It's really rude to have to be an adult. You're telling me I have to go out there and earn my own money, look after myself, *and* I'm responsible for my own happiness? WTF?

I'm in my 30s, and I still want to throw tantrums and stomp my feet like a little child. I'm writing this book, imparting the wisdom that comes from years of medical experience and the absolute hell of going through my own spiritual evolution, creating a whole ass *business* for helping people, and I'm like, this adult shit is just so fucking rude. Why must I have all of these adult responsibilities?

And yeah, I get it's all part of the process, and I'm following my calling, and blah, blah, blah. But you can't tell me I'm the only person who thinks it's rude that we have to act like grown ups all the time. In fact, I say, let's not. If you want to lay down on the floor and kick and scream like you're a toddler having a fit, DO IT. Stomp your feet, punch a pillow, throw a tantrum. So many of us parentified children never actually got to be a child. We had to grow up way too young.

This is my genuine advice: Take yourself to a rage room. You know those rooms where they put you in a hazmat suit and give you goggles and a hammer and you can smash shit into smitherins? Go there and have a genuine tantrum like you've never had before. Give your inner child the tantrum they've always wanted, this time with zero repercussions.

The first time I went, it was with a friend. I was still in a kind of freeze state: disconnected from my anger, dissociated, not fully able to access what was boiling beneath the surface. But the next few times I went, it was alone. It was like an hour of somatic therapy. I was yelling in Punjabi, smashing plates, breaking bottles. It was so cathartic.

Honestly I think rage rooms should be prescribed by doctors. I'm serious. Once a month, minimum. Just like you'd get a massage or a therapy session or go smash shit. Your body *will* thank you.

It reduces inflammation, autoimmune flare-ups, and stress. Buried anger and resentment are slow poisons. You can even bring your own stuff to break. I do. Old plates, empty glass bottles. I keep a little stash now of things I'm saving up for my next session. The last time I went, the staff laughed and said, "She came prepared," because I brought in my own bag of chaos—dishes, glassware, all of it. I was ready. And I didn't just feel lighter after, I felt more like me.

There's a deeper layer to this too, especially if you've dealt with abandonment wounds, particularly through the maternal line. In Family Constellations, the mother is central because we literally come out of her body. And when you've experienced maternal abandonment, or even perceived it, that wound may show up later as learned helplessness.

Even now as an adult, I sometimes forget how much power I have. I'll go into a freeze state when I'm overwhelmed. I shut down, convinced in the moment I can't help myself. It doesn't matter if I have money, therapy, community support, whatever. At that moment, I regress. My body believes I'm dying, that I can't regulate, that I'm completely alone. That's learned helplessness. And my coach pointed it out to me recently, she said, "You're not helpless anymore, Meher. You're an adult."

The rage room, for me, has become a place to actively reject helplessness. A place to remember that I am no longer a child being punished for anger. I'm an adult. I have free will. No one is going to lock me up, shame me, or call me a bad girl for feeling my rage. And it's so freaking good for me too, to be able to express my anger in a safe space. It helps move all of this stuck frozen energy inside of my body and nervous system.

THE IMPORTANCE OF SAFE CONNECTION

Accountability is the hardest thing about healing. It's so damn hard to take honest accountability and not beat yourself up. It's important to take this work gently. You need to hold space for yourself and look at your shadow with compassion. And that is so much easier done when you have trusted connections. When your personal inner critic is too loud, ask for help. Ask for objective feedback because you may have your trauma-tinted glasses on and may not be able to see clearly.

Trauma truly distorts your perception of reality. And I don't mean in this way of deliberately manipulating things to seem worse than they are. But because you're so hurt, your pain is warping your perception. So you need to find someone that you trust and you feel safe with.

The most important element of connection is feeling safe. The way I personally gauge whether someone feels safe is by asking myself if I can share with this person the thing I feel most ashamed about and know they won't judge me for it. I tune into my body for the answer. If the answer is yes, that's how I know it's safe to be vulnerable. If the answer is no, that's my body telling me, not them. Your body will tell you who feels safe and who doesn't.

While solitude and introspection are crucial, especially when you're learning who you are outside the noise of other people's expectations, there's only so far you can go alone. At some point in your healing journey, connection becomes necessary. Whether that's through community, friendship, a therapist, a coach, or attending a workshop, the form doesn't matter. What matters is that you're not doing it in isolation forever. Your version of connection might be a hundred people in a vibrant community, or it might be two or three deeply trusted friends. There's no right answer here. It's about tuning into what feels authentic for you.

Although if you have experienced trauma, I highly recommend finding someone trauma-informed to help you work through those experiences. If you carry a lot of trauma or internalized shame, connection can feel overwhelming for your nervous system. So work through it in bite-sized pieces. You don't need to rip open your vulnerability all at once. Let your guard down slowly and softly, bit by bit.

I can say from personal experience that when you're in the eye of the storm, you can't see your way out. Up until recently, I was in that place myself, telling my coach, "I don't know when this is going to end. Everything still feels so helpless." And the only thing that helped was hearing someone I trust say, again and again, "It will be okay. It will be okay. It will be okay." When you can't hold the faith for yourself, it helps to have someone hold it for you to remind you of how far you have come. It is easy to lose that perspective.

LOVING REMINDER: YOU'RE NOT A CHILD ANYMORE

At some point in your healing journey, you realize this painful, liberating truth: No one is coming to save you. Like the wounded healer can't save her loved ones from their fate, no one else can save you from yours. You need to be your own superhero.

This chapter has asked a lot of you: to be radically honest, to examine the roles you've played, to admit that maybe—just maybe—you've been protecting yourself with resentment or hiding behind pain because it felt safer than change. It suggests you move beyond asking, *What happened to me?* to address instead, *What am I doing with it now?*

And I want you to know: I have nothing but compassion for you in that process. I've been there. I am still there sometimes. But if you want to step into sovereignty, you must be willing to *feel* to truly *heal*. You will feel the grief, the guilt, the tenderness behind your anger, the inner tantrums, and the ache of self-betrayal.

There's a real grieving process to this work. It's important to grieve the loss of the childhood fantasy—the belief that if you just love hard enough, sacrifice enough, do everything right, you can save the people you love. Letting go of that role is not easy. It's painful. And it's absolutely okay to cry about it. Cry in the bath. Cry to your pets. Cry on your therapist's couch while pretending you're "just tired." Whatever works.

There's no expectation that you'll read this and suddenly go, "Oh, I'm not responsible for other people's healing. Cool. Got it. Moving on." No. That would be bypassing the very real grief of letting go.

Grief doesn't come all at once. It comes in layers. It shows up again and again in different forms. One day, you think you've cleared it, and the next month it shows up in a new disguise, asking to be felt all over again. But the point isn't to eliminate the pain; it's to build the capacity to hold it. The point is to grow stronger, to get better at tolerating discomfort, and to hold your pain with tenderness rather than resistance.

I always picture it like this: Imagine a jar with a heavy rock inside. That rock is your grief. It's not going anywhere. You can't remove it. But what you can do is expand the jar. Grow your capacity. Build a bigger container. The grief remains, but the weight feels lighter because you have changed.

Growing your capacity to feel the guilt, the pain, and the discomfort takes time. Get used to radical honesty and holding yourself accountable for the choices you're making. Honesty is the doorway through which you return to yourself. It's the secret key that makes this whole healing thing work. Without it, there is no lasting transformation.

This isn't easy work, but it is sacred. And it's yours to do now with compassion, sovereignty, and deep reverence for the innocent child who carried all of this long before you had words for it. You are your ancestors' prayers.

Honesty is the doorway back to yourself. Without it, healing is avoidance in disguise.

Part 2

PSYCHOLOGICAL
ALCHEMY

CHAPTER 6

HEALING IS RUDE AF!

The most terrifying thing is to accept oneself completely.
–CARL JUNG

Let's just be honest: Healing your shadow isn't easy; it's hard as fuck. It's uncomfortable and rude. It doesn't tap gently on your shoulder, whispering, "Hey honey, it's time to heal," like a kindergarten teacher waking a child up from naptime. It's more like a bloodthirsty UFC fighter that kicks you on your ass, knocking you out cold and bleeding on the floor. As much as I wanted to enter my spiritual awakening like a graceful, incense-burning goddess, there was no grace in my initiation. My awakening started with a heartbreak so humiliating it felt like the Universe had personally slapped me across the face.

I wasn't sure whether I wanted to include this story in my book because it's one of my most mortifying memories. But I want to be honest with you about my journey. And sharing this story here, on these pages, is part of the alchemy; it's how I transmute the shame, reclaim the narrative, and take my power back from a moment that once made me feel powerless. And because alchemy is what this chapter is all about, I decided this story was the perfect illustration.

My humiliating heartbreak occurred during my Saturn return. In astrology, your Saturn return is the period of time when the planet Saturn returns to the same position it was at the time of your birth. It usually happens between ages 28 and 30. It's a period of significant transition and growth, and it's usually recognized by your life completely falling apart especially if you're living a false narrative or identity like I was.

Most of the people I know have had some wild romantic chaos hit during their Saturn return, and mine was no different. Mine started with the first, and last, one-night stand of my life. And to be clear, I didn't *think* it was going to be a one-night stand when we met up that night. I really liked this guy. He was Indian, hot, charming, tall, jacked, and mysterious—you know, all the good stuff on your wishlist. But after our date, things got weird. After we had sex, he casually dropped that he was the son of a billionaire and that he had worked for the CIA in the past. Like, straight-up told me this while we were lying in bed like it was a bad Netflix drama. Then, the next morning, he ghosted me. I searched him on Instagram and found out he was actually an influencer, a romantic coach, of all things. And guess what? Every woman he sleeps with, he posts about her on his social media. That morning, he took a selfie posting number 498 (my number) on his feed as if I was another medal he had acquired.

It felt as if my chest had cracked open. My body felt like it was breaking apart. I was so hurt and humiliated that I couldn't immediately see this moment for what it was: my universal wake-up slap. That moment was the real beginning of my healing journey. Though I didn't know it yet, this was my initiation.

This romantic encounter was the culmination of a series of unfortunate events. I remember thinking, *This is it. This shit keeps happening to me, and now it's so ugly, so humiliating, that I can't ignore it anymore.* I couldn't imagine anything more destructive to my self-worth than this: being reduced to a number on some man's Instagram highlight reel.

And the thing is, my sexuality is sacred to me. I know everyone has their own relationship to sex, and I fully support sovereignty and choice in that. But for me? Sex is a sacred energy exchange. To share that with someone so energetically bankrupt—an energy vampire—was like a spiritual rupture. It ripped me open in a way I couldn't unfeel. That moment forced me to ask: *Why does this keep happening to me?*

My love life was a disaster, and it was such a stark contrast to how competent and powerful I felt in my career. The shame was unbearable. And I remember thinking, *What's the point of having all this success, all this external validation, if I keep giving my power away to men who treat me like I'm disposable?* It was a paradox I'd felt most of my life.

So there I was, lying on my sofa, my body buzzing with grief and rage. It was excruciating. And it was rude. Rude as hell. But it wasn't enough. Even with all the humiliation I felt, I still hadn't been pushed enough to learn the lesson the Universe wanted me to learn. So because I'm a Venus in Scorpio, which means I love deeply and obsess wildly, I went into full stalker mode. I'm not proud of it, but if you've been there, you *know*. I was still obsessing about him six months later, spiraling in the shame of being ghosted. I even emailed him. And when he finally replied, his exact words were: "Geez, you're such a victim."

Let me tell you something: That line gutted me. But it also gave me clarity. There was a shadow part of me that actually agreed that my behavior was like that of a victim. Because as ruthless as he was, I had to face the hard truth that a part of me had attracted that dynamic. I didn't do it consciously, but there was a wound in me that thought I deserved that kind of love. Realizing I held that belief about myself is how I started to take my power back, by taking responsibility. Yes, what happened wasn't my fault, but healing meant looking in the mirror and asking, *What in me allowed this? What in me believed this was all the love I deserved?* That was the beginning of my psychological alchemy. It catapulted my spiritual awakening further and set my entire transformation in motion.

So, what do I mean by psychological alchemy? Let me tell you.

PSYCHOLOGICAL ALCHEMY

Psychological alchemy is the sacred science of falling apart and being reborn. Like a phoenix rising from the ashes of the fire that burnt it down, trauma alchemy is the process of transforming your pain into something sacred, like wisdom, power, and purpose. The name comes from ancient alchemists who tried to turn lead into gold. Trauma alchemy invites us to take the heaviest, most shame-filled parts of our story and transmute them into something that can heal us and serve us and the world.

This kind of transformation isn't about pretending the trauma never happened. It's about facing it, feeling it, integrating it, and refusing to let it define you. Let it *initiate* you. When held with sacred intention, trauma becomes a raw material that you can work with, reshape, and refine until what remains is pure gold. This is a lifelong process and commitment.

Just as the alchemists of ancient times worked to turn lead into gold, our pain can transmute into something beautiful and powerful that can take us to the next level of our journey. But that sort of transformation doesn't come without work. To transform the shit moments of your life into something glittery, you need:

- Radical self-honesty and deep inner work
- Shadow integration (confronting the unconscious parts of yourself)
- Ancestral healing (releasing inherited wounds and patterns)
- Creative expression (through art, writing, music, movement)
- Somatic release (allowing the body to process held emotions)
- Spiritual insight (finding meaning and soul lessons within the pain)

In other words, when you face your trauma and commit to transmuting it into something new, your pain becomes your portal. The heartbreak I experienced crushed me, but the alchemy began the moment I stopped blaming him and started listening to what my pain was trying to teach me. I took accountability for the part of me that attracted this experience.

In the ancient sense, this concept draws from Hermetic alchemy—a spiritual tradition practiced by mystics in Egypt, Greece, Persia, and medieval Europe. While they didn't use the word "trauma," their process was clearly a code for inner transformation. They sought to turn the base metal of human suffering into the gold of enlightenment.

Their teachings highlight four stages of the healing journey:

1. **Nigredo** *(Blackening)* – The dark night of the soul. This is the trauma, the breakdown, the descent into chaos, grief, and the dissolution of the false ego.

2. **Albedo** *(Whitening)* – The purification. Here, light begins to return. This is where self-awareness begins, along with detoxification and spiritual cleansing.

3. **Citrinitas** *(Yellowing)* – The illumination. You gain insight and clarity from what you endured. You begin to reclaim purpose.

4. **Rubedo** *(Reddening)* – The final integration. Spirit and matter unite. You embody what you've learned and become the medicine.

That night with the influencer wasn't just a romantic disaster; it was my Nigredo, the blackening. We were destined to cross Paths, in one of my first dark night of the soul moments. It was the first slap that forced me to look at my patterns and ask,

What keeps me choosing this? The Hermetic principle says, *As above so below, as within, so without.* What you alchemize on the inside shows up in how you live, love, lead, and create on the outside. The ancient alchemists believed that by evolving the self, you contribute to the evolution of the world.

And get this: Ancient societies didn't consider alchemy as mysticism. It was science. In fact, it was the MOTHER of modern chemistry and physics. Before science stripped away the soul/spiritual aspect of transformation, alchemy was a spiritual science practiced across ancient Egypt, India, China, and beyond.

As time passed, the mystical layers were stripped away. By the 1600s and 1700s, alchemy had evolved into chemistry. Alchemists like Paracelsus and Robert Boyle became pioneers of modern science. Boyle's *The Sceptical Chymist* is actually considered a bridge between metaphysics and scientific method. And eventually, by the 1700s and beyond, those same alchemical ideas laid the foundation for physics: the search for universal energy, the exploration of vibration, and the concepts of transmutation that now echo in quantum theory and particle physics.

Science says we have to see it to believe it. Spirituality says we have to believe it to see it. Magic happens when you combine both. Here's the core truth: Alchemy was never pseudoscience. It was protoscience plus metaphysics *plus* soul work. And ironically, modern physics is now circling back— through quantum mechanics, frequency medicine, and energy healing—to the very mysticism it once tried to escape.

Real healing is both a science and a sacred art. When your trauma is tended with courage, curiosity, and compassion, it has the potential to become glittering gold. Sharing the story of my one-night stand and vulnerably writing it down here, offering it to you without flinching, is part of how I keep turning my own spiritual lead into something luminous.

So how do we alchemize our pain? There is no one way. You'll likely come across many modalities on your healing journey, and I invite you to discern which methods call out to you the most. But here are eight modern-day tools I'd like to share to help you begin your own alchemical transformation.

TOOL #1: BE CURIOUS

I'll be honest, I didn't start out curious. My journey started with obsession, shame, and spiraling. It started with lying on my sofa, feeling like I'd been slapped and the giant handprint of the Universe was still stinging on my face. But eventually, I got tired of the pain, and I started asking why. *Why the fuck does this keep happening to me?*

Alchemy begins at rock bottom: the Nigredo phase. The ego death. The part where everything falls apart and nothing makes sense. It is messy and ugly. It's grief, chaos, and collapse. It's your identity breaking under the weight of truth. But buried inside the rubble is the first flicker of light, the first spark. And that spark is curiosity. It comes from the moment you stop numbing and start *noticing*. Curiosity is what begins to shift us out of shame and into self-inquiry.

Being curious means getting to know yourself in a real, unfiltered way. What do you actually like? What triggers you? What patterns show up when you feel abandoned, ashamed, or unseen? When you choose curiosity over criticism, you stop asking, *What's wrong with me?* and start asking, *What is this emotion showing me about myself? What is the deeper soul invitation here?*

That one shift will change your entire life.

The next time you feel angry—especially if it's disproportionate or irrational—take a pause. Observe the emotion as if you were looking at it from above, like an eagle circling. Don't judge or shame it. Just witness it.

Sometimes, you learn more about yourself from what you dislike than what you like. Your disgust, your resentment, your irritability are all feedback. To share a personal example: I used to hate people-pleasers. Hated them. Until I realized it wasn't *them* I hated; it was the part of *me* that learned to survive through people-pleasing.

The phenomenon of disliking in others what one unconsciously sees in oneself is rooted in psychology. Freud called this projection. It's a defense mechanism where individuals attribute their own unacceptable or uncomfortable thoughts, feelings, or impulses to someone else. Jung also talked about this and called it the shadow self. I mentioned in the introduction, and it's worth repeating here, that Jung said everything that irritates us about others can lead us to an understanding of ourselves. When we encounter these traits in others, it can trigger a strong negative reaction because they reflect aspects of ourselves that we haven't accepted or integrated.

At the end of the day, it's all just information. Once you start noticing your reactions and get curious about them, you can move forward thinking, *Awesome, let me integrate this.* When you do, you start to cultivate greater self-awareness, can build better relationships, and reduce overall negativity in your life. But let me be real: it took me two years of conscious work to even use the word "awesome" about this kind of growth.

And remember to honor whichever stage you currently are in. You're not meant to have all the answers yet. Sounds cliché but you are exactly where you are meant to be on your healing journey. You just need to be open to finding them. This is the part where you put on your little scientist hat and start observing your life for data. Ask, *Why is this happening to me?* And listen to what comes up.

The first alchemical ingredient in your transformation is noticing what hurts, asking why, and choosing to stay with the question rather than abandoning yourself all over again.

TOOL #2: CONSTELLATIONS WORK

This is also an important stage in the book to mention Systemic and Family Constellations again. Working with a skilled practitioner during this dark, chaotic, destabilizing period can provide insight into how much of it truly belongs to your ancestors, and which burdens are truly yours to release in order to move forward.

Let me give you a hypothetical example. Let's say you keep getting betrayed in relationships; no matter who you choose, they end up cheating on you. Or to flip it, maybe you're the one who ends up betraying. You might have no conscious awareness of the hidden dynamic driving this. Then you work with a trauma-informed Family Constellations practitioner and step into the field, only to discover there was a half-brother or half-sister you never knew existed. A parent had an affair, and that child was the result. In the soul of a marriage union, that's considered a deep betrayal. What looks like self-sabotage on the surface may actually be the greater soul—the field—demanding equilibrium and restoring order for a forgotten family member. Now before you start playing Sherlock Holmes and digging up hidden family secrets to piece together your life, I *wholeheartedly* urge you to work with a trained, experienced professional to uncover these dynamics safely.

Systemic and Family Constellations can be deeply triggering and even retraumatizing, so I cannot stress enough the importance of working with someone you trust, someone truly aligned to hold space for you. My intention with this book is to help restore love and order in lineages and families, not to spark conflict or fuel blame toward your parents. If anger or rage does come up, it is 100% valid. Just make sure you have a somatic practitioner to help you process that energy. This is how you step into sovereignty: individuating while still belonging to your family system.

TOOL #3: FEEL YOUR FEELINGS

If I could tattoo one healing truth onto your soul, it would be this: You can't heal what you don't feel. Period.

treated like a liability and intuition is labeled "delulu." We're expected to perform, produce, and keep our shit together. We're trained to reward the mind over the body, and when we fall into that mindset, we're going to lack self-trust.

This brings me to reason number three: lack of self-trust. When you start your healing journey, you won't trust yourself or your body. You'll second-guess your anger, gaslight your sadness, and sabotage your joy.

In my case, anger was the emotion I got punished for the most when I was a child. It took me years of deconditioning to realize that anger is sacred. It's the animal in you saying *grrrr*, my boundary is being violated. But when you're told not to be "a bad girl," not to make noise, not to cause problems, you learn to shove that anger deep down inside of you with no vent for it to escape. Remember what I said way back in the introduction about how emotions are energy? When you push anger down and ignore it, that anger doesn't disappear, it remains stuck, transforms into shame, self-hatred, people-pleasing, and burnout. Freud said depression is anger turned inward.

The more you abandon your feelings, the more you break trust with your inner self. Eventually, you go from suppressing emotions to not believing in them at all. You're sad, but you smile. You're furious, but you apologize. You're exhausted, but you keep performing.

THE ONE-MINUTE TIMER PRACTICE

A while back, I found myself dissociating. All. The. Time. So I got curious and asked myself, *What is one thing I could do every day that might help me come back to my body?*

I started setting a timer on my phone every day for just one minute and named it Feel Your Feelings. When it went off, I'd stop what I was doing, close my eyes, take a few deep breaths, and ask: *How am I feeling right now?* I'd notice any sensations in my body or acknowledge the *absence* of sensation. And that was it. One minute. It wasn't anything fancy, but that one minute changed my life.

It created neural pathways in my brain to start checking in with my body again. Over time, I could tell instantly whether my body was clenched or relaxed, whether I was grounded or dissociating. It built a bridge between my mind and my soma. And when you do that every day—even for just sixty seconds— you slowly widen your window of tolerance. Feeling into your feelings becomes more comfortable.

It's through knowing how to understand what your body is telling you, what your emotions are telling you, that you can learn to trust yourself. You learn how to discern. You get to know the language of your intuition.

So if feeling your feelings terrifies you, start slow. Set a timer for one minute and try to feel just *one* emotion. Allow yourself to feel emotions in safe places. Cry in the shower. Scream into a pillow in your bedroom. When I was processing grief, I used somatic meditations on YouTube designed for that specific emotion. When I was angry, I listened to music that helped me *move* the rage through dancing and shaking my body. Try it out for yourself and notice the small shifts!

When you feel your feelings, you stop running from the truth. You bring the light back in, and reconnect to your body. It is in this that you restore your trust within yourself so you can continue on your healing journey.

TOOL #4: CREATE SAFE SOCIAL SUPPORT

There's a moment in healing when you realize you can't do it alone. That moment is terrifying, especially if trauma has taught you that people are unsafe. The world can't be trusted. When you've experienced trauma, you may develop a habit of poor energetic boundaries and you might attract energetic vampires like I did. But here's the truth: Healing doesn't happen in isolation. Healing happens when we are seen, when we are heard, and when we feel safe enough to let someone witness the parts of us we were taught to hide. The key to healing is in finding the people who can offer you safe social support.

For me, that shift started with my mentor, Dr. Schwarz.

Dr. Schwarz was my attending physician during my psychiatry residency. He was the first person—and I mean the very first person—to look me in the eye and say he was truly sorry for what I'd been through with my mom.

I still remember the exact moment. We were in the psych ward, and a patient's mom had come to visit. We watched them walk down the hallway together, and Dr. Schwartz mentioned that he was jealous of the patient. When I asked him why, he said he wished his mother were alive and he could take a walk with her. Without skipping a beat, I said, "Well, mine has schizophrenia." For a moment, Dr. Schwartz didn't say anything, then he looked me in the eyes and said, "I'm sorry."

I remember thinking how interesting that was. No one had ever apologized after I mentioned my mother's condition to them. And it wasn't like a pity apology either. He didn't analyze me or reframe it. He didn't try to fix it or tell me to look on the bright side. He just acknowledged it. The way he said, "I'm sorry," he was also saying, "Damn. That's a lot. That's really significant." And for the first time, I felt something settle in my nervous system. Someone else was showing me empathy for my situation, and I felt seen in a way I hadn't realized I needed. Dr. Schwartz was my first safe social connection, and having that sparked something new in me: a belief that maybe connection didn't have to hurt.

Human connection has felt unsafe for me since I was in utero. Shortly after my birth, my mother was diagnosed with psychosis, and during my first three years she also struggled with alcohol use. Since I had to protect myself from the very person who gave me life, attachment felt dangerous and threatening. There were times, in states of psychosis, when my mom would say we should all take cyanide and die. This is one extreme example of how unsafe it felt for her to be alive in this world because of her illness. For a long time, I used weed to escape my pain, numb myself, and dissociate from my body. What started as recreational use in my 20s became a daily coping mechanism. I felt ashamed and saw it as a moral and personal failure.

As Dr. Gabor Maté has said in his lectures, instead of asking someone, "Why the addiction?" we should ask "Why the pain?" That question really stuck with me. Looking back, I have much more compassion for myself, understanding my marijuana use as a substitute for human intimacy and safe connection. Honestly, given my family history, I'm surprised it wasn't harder drugs.

Here's the thing about safety: It will probably feel boring, especially if your nervous system is addicted to chaos, substances, trauma bonding, or anxiety. Those of us with deep trauma have been conditioned to confuse nervous system dysregulation with chemistry. But excitement isn't always intuition. Don't ever confuse jitteriness about someone new as a message from your soul saying, yes, this person is for you. Most of the time, safety feels neutral. It doesn't come from that person who gives you constant butterflies. It's peaceful, like an exhale you didn't know you were holding.

That's why one of the most important questions to ask yourself when you're around someone is:

Does my body feel safe with them? At this point, you've learned to tune into your body and emotions. You can tell if your body feels relaxed, grounded, and present in their presence.

When you're operating from unhealed trauma, you're likely to either put up energetic walls and isolate or attach to people who aren't safe. This is because trauma causes fear, and fear makes us hypervigilant. It's not your fault. Your nervous system is trying to protect you. But eventually, if you want to heal, you have to rebuild trust, and that begins with learning to trust your body again.

People with trauma often have poor energetic boundaries. We either over-give, over-share, and let everyone in, or we become avoidant and convince ourselves that connection is a weakness, so guarding walls go up instead of healthy boundaries. Ask yourself with honesty (and no shame):

- Am I isolating because I need to protect myself or because I feel shame around seeking support?
- Am I setting boundaries from self-love or as a trauma response?

TOOL #5: SEEK TRAUMA INFORMED PROFESSIONAL HELP

If you can't tell what safety feels like, that's okay. You might be early in your healing. Get professional help. Work with a somatic coach or trauma-informed therapist who can co-regulate with you. Find that safe social connection from trained professionals.

You have to learn to protect your energy and stay open to connection. I call this phase energy vampire rehab. You start recognizing who drains you and who restores you. You get more intentional with your time. You stop trauma bonding with people who only know how to connect through pain. You start gravitating toward people who can hold you, mirror your wholeness, and not get entangled in your wounds.

And yes, that means your old social circles might shift. Some friendships will fade and fall out of alignment. Some relationships won't survive your healing. That's normal. When you stop abandoning yourself, you stop tolerating others who abandon you too. You know you're on the right path when the cost of self abandonment becomes too high. You either say

NO to unaligned opportunities now or your body will set the boundary for you later.

You need to know that safe people exist. Safe love exists. Safe connection is possible. You might not believe it yet. That's okay. Just start by noticing what feels safe in you. Then let that inner knowing lead the way. Sometimes all it takes is one safe and trusted person to begin trusting the world and opening up your heart again.

TOOL #6: BE PATIENT

Let me just say it: I hate this step. I suck at it. Patience is not my strong suit. If healing were a DoorDash order, I'd be standing at the window screaming, "Where is it?" ten minutes after pressing "confirm." And yet…this is the key.

In alchemy, this is the Rubedo phase and we'll talk more about it in Part 3. This is the final transformation: where all the purification, grief, awareness, and insight begins to stick. You become the gold through embodying the process. You stop chasing the healing and learn that you *are* the medicine. I am still working on this right beside you, my dear.

Healing, embodiment, growth, all these things take time. Healing doesn't happen on your ego's timeline. It happens on Saturn's.

Now, you spiritual girlies who follow astrology already know what I'm talking about. Saturn is the planet of time, structure, karma, and patience. It's the slow teacher. It's the old loving father, teaching you the importance of discipline, structure, and overcoming challenges. In Jungian psychology and astrology, the Saturn return (around age 28-30) is when true individuation begins; this is when you truly start becoming an adult.

Saturn says, "You want depth? Cool, prove it. You want wisdom? You'll earn it. You want a soul-level transformation? You'll be initiated through trials, delays, detours, and discomfort. But if you stay the course, walk the path with integrity, and do the damn work, you will be rewarded." It rains diamonds on Saturn. That's not just a metaphor, it's an actual astronomical fact. But we can use it as a metaphor for how Saturn rewards aligned work.

Saturn gets a bad rap in the astrological community, and I don't agree with that narrative. Our rising sign is our life task or life purpose. As an Aquarius Rising, my traditional ruler is Saturn. I have my mixed feelings about Saturn on the heavy days too, but I also see it as a loving father figure who wants me to grow up and learn responsibility and patience. In a world where spiritual teachers and gurus are selling "quantum leaps" and "10x your manifestation" shortcuts, it's easy to forget Saturn's old-school wisdom: delayed gratification for lasting results.

So I try to remember that when things feel unbearably slow. When the vision is clear but the results haven't caught up. When I'm in between timelines and my ego is spiraling, whispering, *You're behind. You're failing. You should've healed this by now,* I breathe and ask: *Does it really matter if it takes me until 40, or 50, or 60 to become the woman I came here to be?* No. It doesn't.

This is the part of healing where you stop performing progress. You stop rushing. You stop trying to force the next breakthrough. You start trusting that the integration is already happening, even when it's invisible. You stop needing every discomfort to come with a download. You let things marinate. And weirdly, life starts to feel more livable.

TOOL #7: CONNECTING WITH YOUR INNER CHILD

One of the ways I practice patience now is by looking forward to things that bring me joy. It helps the time pass in a way that feels nourishing. Take a workshop, dance, book a trip or retreat, cuddle your dogs every day. Find joy every single day because joy gives your healing something to rest against. Quick fun fact: In astrology, your 5th house is where your inner child lives. Look at where it is in your chart and find its ruler; this is the part of your natal blueprint that connects you to the wisdom and creativity of your inner child.

TOOL #8: INVEST IN YOUR BODY, BABE

Let me be real with you: If you want to go the distance with this work, you have to invest in your body. That doesn't mean you need a twelve-step biohacking routine and a personal chef. It does mean you need to honor your body as the vessel of your soul. Because this body—this sacred, sensitive, resilient meat suit—is the thing that's going to carry you to every single one of your earthly material desires.

So get the massage. Book the acupuncture. Take the Epsom salt bath. Move your body. Insist on 9 hours of beauty sleep every night. Nourish yourself by eating organic and clean. Get your nails done if that's your version of ritual. It all counts. One of my mentors, Mia, spends what most people spend on rent to take care of her body. And honestly, that's the wealthiest flex I've ever seen. What's the point in slogging yourself to seven figures if you burn out, get cancer, or have no energy left to enjoy it?

Real wealth isn't just money, it's health. It's nervous system regulation. It's having the energy to make love, dance, travel, rest, and connect. It's being well enough to receive the life you're working so hard to build. So that's what we're really unlocking here: capacity. We're growing our ability to take in more pleasure, intimacy, and joy.

That's what alchemizing your trauma ultimately does; it returns you to yourself. It helps you hold more life. It's your transformation to wholeness, to your ability to follow your purpose, and to live out your life's potential.

TRANSFORMING PAIN INTO EMPOWERMENT

These eight steps sound simple. But let's not pretend this process is linear. Healing doesn't happen in clean, color-coded stages. It's not a Pinterest morning routine. Like a toddler coloring on the walls, the lines are all over the place. Some days, you're deep in curiosity and compassion. Other days, you're rage-crying on the bathroom floor, googling "how to sage a man out of your aura."

The truth is you're going to revisit the same wound in a deeper layer, again and again. But remember, two steps forward, one step back is still one step forward. Progress isn't always visible. But it's there.

In the next chapter, we'll zoom out from the trauma trenches and look at the bigger cosmic force of energy. You'll learn how to recognize the forces of masculine and feminine energy, how to integrate them, and how they've shaped your relationship with trauma.

CHAPTER 7

DANCING WITH THE DIVINE

The masculine mind is in search of the feminine soul.
–CARL JUNG

People tend to argue about how to define masculinity and femininity. They draw hard lines in the sand to dictate what fits in which category: blue is for boys, pink is for girls. Although this paradigm is shifting, with gender being recognized as more fluid. However, traditionally viewed men are logical, and women are emotional. And yes, when we look at these energies through a spiritual lens and traditionally, masculinity is defined by the mind, intellect, and logic. And femininity is associated with the heart, emotion, and intuition. But that's not the end of the story.

No matter what spiritual background you have, I think we can agree that masculine energy is protective in nature. But that doesn't mean that feminine energy isn't as protective, if not more so, under the proper circumstances. Have you ever turned on the Animal Planet, National Geographic, or Discovery Channel? You've seen how protective a mama bear can be when her cub is threatened? She will rear up on her hind legs and roar as if she's saying to the predator, "I will destroy you." It's pure feminine rage as sacred protection.

On the flip side, we often associate feminine energy with softness and nurturing, but that doesn't mean masculine energy can't nurture too. Think of a father cradling his newborn baby at 3 a.m., gently rocking them back to sleep with fierce tenderness in his tired arms. Sure, there is a protective energy there, but he's also emotionally present, attuned, loving and holding space, which are all considered feminine traits.

Let me tell you a story.

When I went to Peru for what was called a Sacred Sisters Retreat, I assumed it would be all women. I mean, that's what the title Sacred Sisters suggested. But when we arrived, there was a man there, Papá, a shaman, sitting with us in our so-called sacred women's circle. And I was initially pissed. Not only because I felt blindsided that a man was present (though that too), but because a week earlier, one of my sexual abuse memories had resurfaced. I showed up to the retreat in an emotionally raw space, hyperaware of my surroundings, and defensive around masculinity.

We should have been told a man would be present in a woman's space. At the same time, I fully believe that this was happening for a deeper reason right around the full moon in Scorpio. Even though I initially didn't like it, I rolled with it.

I ended up having to leave Peru three days before the retreat's scheduled close, but before I left, I did a hapé ceremony with Papá. He agreed to do it a day early, just for me, so I didn't miss it. When I arrived in the ceremonial space, he had his 5-year-old son in his lap. They sat together like that for four hours—his son curled into his body while he administered the plant medicine. And he wept. This man cried more than any other woman I'd met on that retreat.

He talked about the grief of losing his father. The grief of separating from his wife. The grief of how masculinity had wounded his lineage. He also talked about love. "I tell my son every day how much I love him," he said. "Every day."

I looked at this man with tears streaming down his face, holding his son close, facilitating sacred healing work, and I thought, *How can anyone say masculinity isn't love? That love belongs to the feminine alone?*

We are often quick to collapse masculinity into coldness, but real masculinity has heart. Real masculinity is love.

My father is one of the most masculine men I know. He's also one of the most compassionate human beings I've ever met. I'm not saying that because he's my dad. I truly mean it. I've never seen anyone love like he does. His compassion is not about people-pleasing or needing to be liked or any other performative reason. It's natural, and it's endless like a well of outpouring that never runs dry.

I aspire to have the kind of compassion my father does. But to be honest with you, I don't always *get* it. I asked him, "How can you be such a giver?" I've seen it in others where that kind of giving creates a martyr or quiet inner resentment somehow. But with him, he does it in a way that's beautiful. In a way I haven't learned how to do, yet.

So you can't tell me masculine energy isn't capable of deep, overwhelming, breathtaking love. And yes, same with the feminine. But the point isn't to rank them or divide them or say which one loves more. It's to stop acting like one holds the heart while the other holds the sword. Love is both.

How about we stop putting masculine and feminine energy in separate boxes like they're opposing teams. These aren't two warring factions neatly divided by some divine gender line. These energies bleed into one another.

You are both masculine and feminine energy. I am both masculine and feminine. We are all both. Believing we are only one or the other is a spiritual error. This is important to know because true healing requires both the structure and safety of the masculine and the emotional flow and connection of the feminine working together, in unison, inside us.

SACRED POLARITY

Let's get something straight: When I talk about masculine and feminine energy, I'm not talking about men and women. I'm not talking about genitals or how you perform in society. I'm talking about divine polarity. The primordial dance of creation that's happening in everything—from minuscule organisms to your deepest spiritual initiations.

What I'm talking about here isn't New Age. This shit is a tale as old as time. The ancients knew this long before Instagram started debating "alpha males" and "soft girl eras." In Hermetic philosophy, it's called the Principle of Gender. It's the seventh and final law in *The Kybalion*, which states:

"*Gender is in everything; everything has its Masculine and Feminine Principles; Gender manifests on all planes.*"[12]

So what does that actually mean?

It means that masculine and feminine energies are the building blocks of the Universe. These two energies are interwoven without binary. Every plane—mental, physical, emotional, spiritual—contains both. You, me, the cosmos, your nervous system, your business plan, your next orgasm: They are all the result of creation from both.

Masculine energy is active. It's the part of you that initiates, sets direction, and holds discipline. This is the energy of action. Feminine energy is receptive, nurturing, and creative. It's the part of you that listens, gestates, and allows. This is the energy of surrender.

Nothing gets born without both. The masculine plants the seed while the feminine brings it to life. The masculine is the spark of the idea, and the feminine is what holds it, nourishes it, and eventually these two manifest it into physical form. Intention without embodiment or aligned action is a fantasy. Surrender without direction is collapse.

If you've ever had an intention or idea (masculine) that needed time, space, and feeling (feminine) to become something real,

---

12 Three Initiates, *The Kybalion,* Gender, (Chicago: Yogi Publication Society, 1908), chap. 15.

then you've already experienced embracing both energies. If you've ever tried to manifest something from pure force without letting yourself feel it first, then you've seen what happens when one energy tries to dominate the dance.

This principle is not about becoming more feminine or more masculine. It's about learning how to marry them inside of you. If you're only operating from one of these energies, or if you've been taught to reject one because of trauma, culture, or conditioning, you're probably out of balance.

To heal, you need to allow the feminine to bring the wound to the surface where there is space to grieve and transmute. You also need the masculine to stay present with it, to protect the process, to give it direction and containment so it doesn't drown you.

When I was suicidal, it was my masculine energy that saved me. My masculine was the part of me that rose up like a warrior and kept fighting for my precious life. It saved me because it loves me so much. It wanted to keep me alive. It was my protection mechanism that engulfed me while the feminine energy brought up all the years of underlying emotions of years with unprocessed grief, pain, and trauma. I mention this because I want any women reading this who have ever felt "too masculine" to know that masculinity is saving your damn life. It really does love you.

Without the masculine, you spiral. If you only engage feminine energy (emotional openness, flow, or chaos) without the masculine to hold it, you may become overwhelmed, lost in emotion, or stuck in cycles of retraumatization. And without the feminine, you bypass. If you only rely on masculine energy (logic, discipline, control), you risk avoiding your emotions entirely. You rely on intellectualization as a crutch and avoid actual healing bypassing the body. Healing happens when feminine energy invites the pain to the surface, and masculine energy stays grounded and present enough to help you move through it without collapsing.

WHEN ONE ENERGY IS WOUNDED, SO IS THE OTHER

As you're reading this, you've probably got a pretty good idea of which energy you naturally lean into more. When you realize that you've been suffocating one energy, the natural inclination is to overcorrect. "I'm done being in my masculine. I'm only soft now." Or: "Feeling is weakness, I'm staying focused and productive." But when one energy is wounded, the other one doesn't get to thrive.

If there is one thing from this chapter, it's this: These energies don't operate in isolation. They are partners. So if you're carrying trauma, odds are both your inner masculine and feminine have taken a hit.

Let me give you a personal example.

My father is the definition of a masculine provider. He built an empire from the ground up. He was born into nothing and rose to everything, accumulating power, success, leadership, and wealth. When my mother got sick, he accepted his fate and buried his pain and grief. He kept showing up, continued building his empire, and always held it together. Never once did I see him break. He carried the masculine ideal of "I have to stay strong for the family," and in doing so, he never let himself feel the loss that was battling underneath.

My mother is the opposite. She embodies pure feminine energy in the sense that she feels deeply. She's spiritual, intuitive, and generous. But she's also completely ungrounded. She struggles to take action. She can't discern what's real from what's imagined. I believe she suffers from a spiritual version of psychosis. It's what happens when our third eye is wide open, but our root chakra is completely blocked; we are ungrounded and imbalanced. So she's totally connected to another dimension, a different reality, and she's not grounded in the earthly plane. My mother gets overwhelmed by her emotions and struggles to ground her gifts in reality. Her emotions are sometimes like a storm, but there's no container. There is no inner structure.

As a product of the two of them, I inherited both of their patterns. Their imbalances became mine. I became hypermasculine in some areas—rigid, driven, emotionally armored—because I rejected the chaotic softness I saw in my mother. But I also carried her fate: the depression, grief, and emotional sensitivity.

Family Constellations teaches that the parent you consciously reject externally, you embody internally. The energy you idolize often becomes your survival strategy. The one you reject becomes your shadow. So, even though I tried to model my father's strength, I still ended up drowning in the depression my mother battled with most of her life.

It doesn't matter which parent you think you're "more like." The one you suppress will find its way into your life. Remember you are both your parents in equal parts; these polarities exist within you. Although an important point to reiterate is that same sex parent trauma is more significant in life struggles and challenges. Their patterns will repeat in your body, your relationships, your triggers, and your symptoms—every time.

Now I'm trying to be more intentional about how I can belong more consciously to my mother. I do this by developing my psychic and spiritual gifts. It's something I'm still working on. I'm still healing. Whether we like it or not, this is a lifelong journey.

Healing means forever asking, *How can I belong to my family in healthier ways? How do I individuate? How do I balance between the two? How can I honor ancestral gifts and strengths, while becoming my own version of an adult and making different choices?*

The thing about finding the balance between energies is you don't have to get it perfect. Like most things in life, you have to start somewhere. It's okay to bounce between masculine and feminine as you figure out how to find that sweet spot between action and surrender.

Perfection is a lie, and striving for it will paralyze your healing. More often than not, if one energy is wounded, the other is too. If you're hypermasculine, chances are there's a wounded feminine underneath that's driving it. If you're hyperfeminine, there's likely a part of you that's scared to step into structure, protection, or clear boundaries.

YOU BECOME WHAT YOU REJECT (SORRY, IT'S SCIENCE AND SPIRIT)

If you're trying to heal your masculine and feminine energy, start close to home. Start with your parents. This is where the biggest shifts happen. Always. As I inherited specific patterns from my mom and dad, you likely inherited some from both of yours. Understanding how their energies shaped you is often the first hint at where you can start to regain balance.

In Family Constellations, you become loyal to the parent you reject. I rejected my mother initially. I wanted to be nothing like her when I was growing up. I also carried a lot of shame around saying this about my own mother retrospectively. I saw her as chaotic, emotionally volatile, unstable, and ungrounded. So I went hard in the other direction: structured, self-disciplined, logical, masculine. I became someone who got shit done. I prided myself on it.

And, yet, somehow, all of the emotional instability I judged in her, I ended up living. The depression, the mental health issues, the spiritual crisis. I unconsciously stepped into the very pain I tried to avoid. That's how loyalty works in the field. Remember as we mentioned in earlier chapters, the field always seeks equilibrium and balance.

The suppressed doesn't disappear just because you don't acknowledge it. It morphs and shapeshifts until it finds a way to slink out of Pandora's box and into your life.

MONEY WOUNDS

Bonus: Want to heal your relationship with money? Constellations can help with this too. In the field, money is seen as love. If there are energetic blockages, ancestral burdens, or enmeshments in your family system, they can interrupt the flow of this unconditional love and life force.

Your relationship with money often mirrors your relationship with your mother. Mom represents your ability to receive abundance from the Universe. Dad represents your ability to keep that money, to build it, and to sustain it. Healing the mother wound, in particular, can transform your relationship with wealth and abundance.

Even Meera, who I've mentioned throughout this book, officially calls herself a trauma-informed ancestral and money coach—the two are that deeply connected.

YOUR LINEAGE IS THE PORTAL, NOT THE PROBLEM

We want to rely on the cosmos or past lives or outside mentors when it comes to healing our past. And sure, all of that has value. But you can move mountains in your family system by restoring order and balance while working with a skilled constellation practitioner. It can start with the energies of just your mother and father.

This isn't about blaming your parents. They did the best they could with the resources they had. The point is to liberate yourself from unconscious burdens so you can move on, grow up, and do the things you came here to do with the beautiful gift of life they gave you. Once you remove these energetic blockages, you can finally let the unconditional love they have for you on a soul level flow to you. So let this infinite source of life force energy flow from your ancestors into you and into all of your creative desires, pursuits. and manifestations.

Masculine and feminine energy were never meant to war inside you. They were meant to love each other and to create through their union.

Healing is never about becoming someone else. It's about becoming more you. And as you do that, you're not only healing your body or your mindset. You're healing your lineage. You're breaking spells that were cast before you ever got here.

But let's be honest: That doesn't always feel good. With that said, the next chapter is about how we get through those dark moments that feel like shit. It's about hitting rock bottom and learning how to survive your dark night of the soul. Let's talk about how depression comes up during the healing process and how to make depression sexy. Or as I call it: #depresexy.

CHAPTER 8

DO DEPRESSED SEXY

I got 99 problems but being sexy solved them all.
−SAHARA ROSE

As much as it sucks, we know we have to go through hell in order to come out stronger on the other side. After learning about psychological alchemy in chapter 6, you now know that hellfire isn't there to burn you; it's there to *forge* you. Still, it's easy to forget that some days, and even if you remember, you might still feel pretty shitty in the moment. The work is about becoming someone who isn't ruled by triggers, wounds, or the ghosts of their lineage—someone who is finally, fully sovereign. You don't get to alchemize into gold without first being willing to melt. And even if you know there's gold on the other side of the breakdown, the melting part still fucking sucks.

In this chapter, I want to dive deeper into the vaults of darkness, the terrifying horrors of the dark night of the soul, the part of the healing process where grief, shame, and rage overtake you. Sometimes you don't know if you'll ever be able to get out of bed again. And I want to show you that not only will you come out of this phase stronger than ever, but you can walk through that dark fire with your head held high, feeling sexy as fuck.

To start, I need to give credit where credit is due. Shout out to my granny! My ability to "do depressed sexy" comes straight from her. She would love that I'm putting this in a book. And honestly, she deserves the recognition. She had *elite* taste. Everything she wore was emerald green. Her jewelry was impeccable. Let me tell you, that lady was a total vibe. And she may not have known a damn thing about boundaries, but what she did know was how to look good while enduring the weight of the world. She helped raise 14 children and still expected to be thanked every time she walked into a room. And maybe she didn't always get the love she deserved, but she sure as hell always got her hair and nails done.

I like to think my nani's (that's how we say grandmother in Hindi) style rubbed off on me. Even in my worst depressive episodes, I still managed to have my nails done, my lashes on, and a blowout booked. Although some days I did appear homeless with unmatched socks and stained pajamas, no judgment!

But it certainly helps that I also have my Venus in Scorpio in the 10th House, the house of career, legacy, and public image. That placement made damn sure I knew how to look good while falling apart. Stressed but well-dressed was my mantra during those periods. Even when my shadow had me crying on the floor, I still looked hot.

POWER AND SEX ARE DEEPLY INTERTWINED

Yes, from the lens of Family Constellations, they truly are. Sexual abuse of all forms and disguises can take your power away. This is especially true if it happened when you were a child who lacked autonomy. So many victims, including me, end up hating themselves. We become ridden with guilt and shame, directing these emotions internally and suppressing the rage of violation. #Depresexy is the art of honoring your pain without letting it define your worth. It's romancing your shadow instead of hiding it. It's walking into the underworld in stilettos and saying, "Fine. If I'm going to suffer, I might as well slay."

Sahara Rose captured it perfectly in her song, "Sexy Dark Night of the Soul," when she said, "I got 99 problems but being sexy solved them all." You've got to strut into the darkness, feeling yourself, knowing that you're about to become the bad bitch your past self always wanted to become.

Shadow periods suck. You're going to fall apart. You're going to cry. You're going to consider giving up everything you worked for that got you this far. But when you learn how to do depressed sexy, you not only survive the darkness, you alchemize it into style, sovereignty, and smolder. One thing that can help you do that is understanding this phase[13] and how to process the trauma you're holding inside. So let's dive in.

---

13 It's important to note that while we call this experience a phase and it comes from the Negrido stage in psychological alchemy, healing is *not* linear. Yes, all things come to pass and you will not be stuck in any period forever, but that does not mean that once you're through the darkness that the darkness will not come again. This is lifelong work, and you will be back to different phases before new ascension periods. Be careful not to stuff your healing into limiting boxes.

WELCOME TO YOUR EGO FUNERAL

Shadow periods have a way of pulling out your curls and smudging your mascara all in the same breath. They don't just humble you. They *annihilate* you. These are the moments when the Universe steps in and says, "Oh, you thought you were in control? That's cute." They're known as Tower moments, ego deaths, or grief portals. Call them what you want. But when they hit, they hit hard.

Everything you've wrapped your identity around starts to fall apart. Your job, your relationship, the dream you were clinging to like it was your lifeline, it's all gone to chaos. You're standing in the ruins, and nothing is what you thought it was. These are the seasons where the identity you've curated—consciously or not—starts to crumble, and you don't know what will be left after the breakdown. That's the whole point. You're in initiation, babe.

Shadow periods are shame-soaked, rage-filled, grief-heavy passages where you question everything, including your own worth. You cry so hard your body trembles. You lie on the floor, belly down, sobbing into the earth like it's the only thing that can hold you. You look around and realize no one is coming to save you. You're on your own. And that's when the real alchemy begins. Then you're forced to either show up or give up.

You can't transform if you're still clinging to your old identity. The old version of you, who needed external validation, who stayed silent to keep the peace, who thought the only way to be safe was to cling to control. That person doesn't make it through the fire. But the woman who rises like a phoenix from the ashes, that bitch is the real you.

IT'S GIVING SPIRITUAL TREND (BUT YOU CAN'T HEAL IN AN INSTAGRAM HIGHLIGHT REEL)

Let's talk about the shadow period—what it actually is, not what Instagram made it look like. Carl Jung called it the dark night of the soul, and let me tell you, he wasn't being metaphorical. These are the times in life when the Universe rips the rug out from under your feet. The moments that come after breakups, job losses, health crises, and deaths.

You are not in control. That's the first truth shadow periods slam you with. They are deeply humbling. You're not just sad. You're grief-stricken, rage-filled even. You're feeling the kind of feelings you've spent a lifetime pushing down so you could keep it all together on the surface. You're in the dark tunnel, the void. And you can't see the light at the end of it.

Now here's the kicker: While all this is happening, the internet is trying to sell you a candle and a journaling prompt so you can get on some influencer's mailing list. Everyone's got their "shadow work moment" posted: aesthetic flat lay, herbal tea, soft music, and a caption about releasing what no longer serves them. I'm not even judging; I make posts like that too. Just a few days ago, I literally posted an Instagram story from Brooklyn with my iced matcha and hot pink shadow work journal like, "If only shadow work was this easy."

But as cute as that looks on your Instagram stories, it's a romanticism of what shadow work really is. I'm not saying that the candles and journal prompts don't help. Creating a ritual where you sit down with your journal and favorite bevy can help uncover some of the surface layers. There is a time and a place for everything. But when you're really in it, shadow work isn't cute. It's primal. It's ugly crying on the floor, face down, snot in the carpet, a Magnolia Bakery cupcake half-eaten next to your grounding mat with chocolate caked in the corners of your mouth. And yes, even when you're crying on the floor with yesterday's eyeliner smudged halfway down your cheeks, that's still a look. You're still #depresexy.

Another thing to understand is that if you've been carrying generations of emotional repression, you can't just sprinkle some glitter on the shit and hope it doesn't stink. The more pain you have, the more you're being asked to put it into the oven so the heat can transmute it into gold. If you're just sprinkling fairy dust on the surface, you're not going to get much return on your healing investment. If you've got a mountain of trauma to process, it's going to take more than a couple of journaling sessions at your local café.

That's why it always comes back to…say it with me: Discernment. Discernment is everything. Shadow work is not about doing something, it's about *feeling* something. It's feeling your emotions that will get them moving. Sometimes the work is to journal. Other times, the work is to scream into a pillow. Or sleep. Or cry. Or eat the damn cupcake. It's intuitive, and it's moment to moment. The question isn't "What should I do?"

It's "What do I need right now?" And then follow whatever instructions your body gives you.

Of course, my favorite way to process unhealed trauma is through Systemic and Family Constellations.

SYSTEMIC AND FAMILY CONSTELLATIONS SAVED MY LIFE (NO, LITERALLY)

There's a reason I keep coming back to Family Constellations. It's because when I was in the thick of my shadow period, it was *the thing* that saved my life.

When I think about how Family Constellations helped me through my shadow periods, this vision comes to my mind where I'm in the middle of an ocean, drowning. I would love to say the ocean is made up of only grief, but there's also shame and fear, and the difficult emotion of never having truly let myself feel any emotion throughout my whole life until this point. But now I feel everything. My ego has been completely cracked open. I'm swimming in this ocean of emotion, and I'm trying for dear life to keep my head above water. Then Meera, my FC coach, comes by me in a row boat, and she throws a rope to pull myself in.

At this point in my life, I'm still holding on to that rope. I'm pulling myself in, and I'm not quite inside the boat yet. But I've survived the storm. I'm still riding the waves of the aftermath, still getting slapped around by the water on occasion, but I got through the worst of it. I'm telling myself that I am safe now.

That's what Family Constellations gave me.

I've mentioned already how so much of the grief, guilt, shame, and trauma that you've been carrying isn't even yours. Family Constellations helps you find the source so you can unhook yourself from it. It makes the invisible visible.

Constellation sessions are held either in groups or one-on-one. In the session, you set up a "living map" of your family system. The facilitator helps you pick other participants or physical objects for various roles and family members. This process is done in a blind fashion to eradicate bias. You don't know who you picked as your mother until later. The other people (or objects) are placed to represent family members, and the unconscious dynamics start to reveal themselves in the room. You begin to feel what's been hidden: the burdens, the entanglements, the loyalties you've inherited without realizing it. You think your anxiety is about your job. But in the constellation, you find yourself standing in your grandmother's grief, carrying her lost child, her silent heartbreak.

Remember, in earlier chapters I mentioned that constellations are based on Orders of Love. The generation who came before you are the bigger ones, and you, my friend, are the little one. Order takes precedence. Just like with your children you are the bigger one and they are the little one. Going against this law is what creates a lot of energetic imbalances in family systems and disrupts the flow of life force energy. When children act like they know what is best for their parents, this is essentially parentification and is doomed to fail because it is the wrong order.

This is where shit gets wild, because once you see the pattern, you can start to unburden yourself from it. Maybe you've been carrying your father's depression because you kept a family secret for him out of loving loyalty. From a broader perspective, your inner child was simply trying to keep the family unit together through an innocent act of love. Or maybe you've stayed small your whole life because shining would mean outgrowing your lineage, and subconsciously, that felt like betrayal.

Systemic and Family Constellations help you return those burdens to their rightful owners. When you do, your life finally starts to feel like yours. Divine order is restored, and it becomes a kind of poetic justice on a soul level. It may sound paradoxical that returning shame, guilt, or any other energetic block you've been carrying actually allows life force energy—and love—to flow again. This process is done with deep honor and respect, not in a "Fuck you, I'm tired of carrying your shit" kind of way.

ORDERS OF LOVE

One of the deepest ways I've had to face this truth of order and hidden burdens in my own life was through my abortion. I wasn't sure if I was going to talk about this, and for most of this book's writing process, I didn't plan to. I thought I would leave it buried in the shadow cage because of my personal fear of facing cultural taboo, especially as an Indian woman. It's not easy to share, and yet, if I'm writing a book about healing shame, then my soul feels called to share this and to bring this shadow into the light too.

There are so many women who carry a secret like mine, especially in cultures like mine, where getting pregnant out of wedlock is taboo. Abortion in many cultures is often surrounded by shame, secrecy, and limited access. We're told to hide it, to lock it away, and in doing so we chain ourselves to shame and karmic debt that lingers for generations.

Three years ago, I had an abortion. When you look at it from the surface level, you might think it was just a medical procedure, something you "move on" from with time. I mean both my partner and I at the time were not ready to be parents. It felt like the right thing to do. But in FC, order matters. And the number one wrong order is when a child dies before a parent. Whether the baby lived a day outside the womb or never made it past the first trimester, that child is still part of the system. When they are not acknowledged, the burden falls on the next generation.

That's how karmic debt works; it doesn't disappear because you pretend it didn't happen. You are essentially taking away the free will of another soul with this choice. And for the love of Christ, this is not me being pro or against abortion, this is simply another level of awareness and knowledge. You 100% have the free will to choose either way. What I emphasize is that when this is swept under the rug, and not acknowledged or given "proper and right order in the field" during a session, someone next in the lineage ends up carrying it.

Order is everything. When order is broken, love cannot flow properly. That's what I want women to understand: Abortion isn't just about the mother's body, it reverberates through the soul and the family system.

For me, the cost was heavy. Since my abortion, I have faced my fair share of karmic debts. On a soul level, it's like a block I've been carrying. I know I'm not alone in that. There are women whose careers don't take off, whose relationships keep failing, whose lives feel stuck. And underneath the struggle is what we call an entanglement in the field, which needs to be acknowledged and given the right order.

Abortions aside, I have seen this rule apply without fail in families where there is a lot of suicide, and the shame that subsequently follows in the family system. The child taking his life before a parent is deceased is again the wrong order, so every next sibling in line is unconsciously going to follow in the deceased child's footsteps. On a soul level, it is again pure love and loyalty, with the family member unconsciously feeling, *After all, who am I to live a full life when you couldn't?* Connecting to my sisters in the field has given me solace and I know they are cheering me on from the other side.

Family Constellations is not about morality; the greater soul does not care about individuals, all it cares about is restoring equilibrium. This further helps us step out of victim/perpetrator dynamics. You may choose to disagree, and respectfully that is your autonomous choice. However, in my humble opinion, we all have been both sides, murdered and the murderer. Both parts live within us.

That's why I'm sharing this story. Because secrets are poison. The shadow is nothing but a shame cage, and the more you keep your secrets locked inside, the more power they have over you. Shame thrives in silence. The moment you speak it aloud in the presence of someone safe (keyword: *safe*), its power dissolves. That's why I want to put this here, in these pages, not only for myself, but for every woman who has been carrying the weight of this in isolation.

This book is special because it's not just about me; it's about healing the women in my lineage, and hopefully helping other women free themselves from the shame cage too. If my story cracks open even one lock in someone's personal Pandora's box, if it helps one woman breathe easier, then it's worth the vulnerability.

One of the most beautiful gifts this work offers is compassion, for both yourself and your family. When you see the whole system—who came before you, what they endured, how much was unspoken—you stop seeing your parents as villains. You stop seeing yourself as broken. In fact you may be surprised and unflattered to find you are not as innocent as you think after all. You start to understand that we've all been tangled in the same web, and we're all trying to find our way home.

Trauma lives in the nervous system. And when you've spent your whole life in a state of hypervigilance, always scanning for emotional landmines, you need to understand your pain. You also need to feel safe enough to release it.

Family Constellations, when done right, in a trauma-informed manner helps the body finally relax. When the system is restored to its natural order—when the lost are honored, the roles are rebalanced, and the truth is named—your body feels it. You breathe easier and something in you feels right when correct order and balance are restored. This is again beyond the limits of logical meaning.

INTEGRATE YOUR HEALING WITH SOMATIC WORK

But let me be clear: FC isn't some lighthearted healing circle with palo santo and affirmations and good vibes only. Family Constellations is intense. It's not safe unless your facilitator knows what the fuck they're doing. Because what it does is rip open trauma loops that have been buried in your lineage for decades, sometimes centuries. You think you're doing a little spiritual exploration, and then suddenly you're face-to-face with your grandmother's abortion grief or your father's unspoken rage, and it's in your body. In one of my first sessions, I felt my great-grandmother's murderous rage pulse through my blood. But that needed to happen. I needed to feel that rage so I could resolve it, so it would no longer impact me.

When I first started learning the method, I was blown away. I thought, *Why doesn't the whole world know about this?* I asked Meera why it wasn't more mainstream. I mean this therapy was literally the diamond of all healing I have ever tried. She told me, "Because for every one good Family Constellations facilitator, there are two bad ones." And those bad ones are out there opening up people's deepest wounds and sending them home with no tools of integration or capacity to process the rage or betrayal they must feel after uncovering a painful family secret. That's why it's so important to find someone who is trauma-informed.

Family Constellations is a powerful medicine. But medicine without the right dosage or container becomes poison. If you're not pairing it with somatic integration, you're ripping the scab off with no plan to stop the bleeding. This work lands in the body, and it has to be processed in the body. Otherwise, you're left dissociated, overwhelmed, and retraumatized.

That's why, in my practice, I'm relentless about pairing this work with nervous system regulation and somatic care. And that can be extremely difficult when you've lived your whole life stuck in your head. When someone asks you for the first time what you're feeling in your body, you may not know how to answer because that kind of thought is brand new.

It's like learning to walk. You need to take baby steps. You need to get inquisitive and think, *Oh, my arm feels like this. My feet are very cold. There's a constriction in my chest. There is a knot in my belly.*

Learning how to communicate how you feel in your body not only helps you come back down into your body, it also helps the practitioner help you with your healing. They can help you unpack those emotions and find where the source is coming from.

When you do this work, you need to go slow. You need somebody who is both trauma-informed and somatically trained to help you process your grief. As you do this work, you will be hit with a tsunami of information as you uncover your unprocessed trauma.

You need to have a guide who can help you slow down so you're not pushing too much. Anytime you go in the direction of pushing, that is the wrong direction for healing. Your nervous system needs to go slow. The slower you go, the more long-lasting your healing will be. Somatic experiencing and processing helps you integrate and move on.

THE GRIT OF GROWING UP

If somatic processing brings you back into your body, then guilt is what brings you back into your humanness. Like I said, its extremely unflattering to take a hard look in the mirror at your shadow behaviors and take accountability to grow the fuck up.

From a Family Constellations perspective, your ability to tolerate guilt is directly tied to your ability to be an adult. And I don't mean adult in the "pay your bills and go to therapy" way. I mean it in a spiritual sense. Becoming an adult means giving up the innocence of childhood and the fantasy that you can be a blameless victim of your circumstances.

This is a freewill planet. There's no judgment here. If you want to stay in the innocence of childhood, you can. No one's keeping score. But if you want to grow, if you want to step into your power, if you want to become the glorious goddess you are destined to be, you're going to have to feel the sting of guilt. You're going to have to tolerate the discomfort of hurting people by doing what's right for you.

I still carry guilt. Sometimes I have to keep my mom blocked on WhatsApp for my own protection. Her paranoia can get intense—she'll message me saying she might be killed or that people are watching us through hidden cameras. Those kinds of messages send shockwaves through my nervous system.

Still, I choose to honor my mother in other ways, like through this book. She's such an educated woman, she even wanted to write a book herself, as I mentioned earlier. I'm grateful to her for my intelligence. She studied for her MBA in marketing while she was pregnant with me. Because of her, I was able to unlock psychic abilities early in life and experience exponential growth. All of that comes from the love that flows from her into me. On a soul level, the love is unconditional. I will always belong to her.

The real question is: *In which ways do you want to belong? Through self-sabotage—or through the ancestral psychic gifts you carry?* As an adult, you get to choose.

Special shout-out to Meera for this one. When I first started Constellation work, I couldn't even look at my apathetic mom in the field. There was so much disconnection. Fast forward a year, and I just got off the phone with my mother, bawling my eyes out after telling her I loved her. I felt irritated that she didn't say it back because she still struggles with dissociation and the numbing from years of antipsychotics. I said, "Mumma, I said I love you," and she responded, "Meher, I love you more than myself." That moment was truly special.

When I was a little girl, my mother couldn't even hold a reciprocal dialogue for two sentences. She was so sick she had to undergo electroconvulsive therapy (ECT) twice. Family members would remind me, "Your mother was electrocuted," in Hindi. It left a real hollow, gaping wound. It used to enrage me. How sick and pathetic it all felt! I would ask, *Why me? Why is my mother the sickest?*

But here's the beauty of healing: I now know, without a doubt, that my soul picked the best mother for me.

In Family Constellations, growing up is the goal. As an FC facilitator, my job isn't to make you feel better. My job is to help you grow up. I don't say that to clients directly, but it's the energy I hold. It's my work behind the scenes. How can I help them exercise their free will more? How can I help them become more conscious? How can I help them shine a light on the hidden gold in their shadow? But as Meera tells me, the field only goes as far as the client is willing to go.

Growing up is the gateway to real healing. Real healing comes from owning your choices, feeling the guilt, and walking forward anyway.

REFRAMING MALADAPTIVE COPING

I used to be incredibly judgmental about addicts. I say that with humility and a lot of hindsight. Back when I was a psychiatry resident, I saw addiction as a weakness.

That's why I love what Dr. Gabor Maté says: "Don't ask why the addiction, ask why the pain." It's profoundly true. It's ultimately the pain that we are all trying to numb and escape from. When I look back at my old self, I can say with love that my mother was in a lot of pain. I'm proud and very sad to look back and see that there was so much pain that I had to numb.I can hold incredible compassion for others going through it because of that.

When I finally allowed myself to get curious instead of judgmental, everything changed. Through Family

Constellations, I learned that recreational drugs are often a sign of a child missing their father on a soul level. Hard drugs are often an unconscious "fuck you" to the mother because the body comes from her. Addiction, in this context, is the opposite of true connection and a replacement for real intimacy.

When you stop shaming your coping mechanisms and start seeing them as clues from your shadow, you stop trying to "fix" yourself and can find the root of the pain.

YOU MIGHT BE DEPRESSED, BUT YOU'RE STILL HOT AS HELL

If there's one thing I hope you walk away with from this chapter, it's this: You don't have to wait to feel better before you start honoring yourself. You can be grieving and glamorous, tears streaming down your face and still know how to shake your ass in the mirror, your full body radiating sacred feminine power. You can do depression sexy.

#Depresexy is a radical act of self-love. It's the ability to honor your pain without losing your dignity. To refuse to allow shame to keep you small and obedient. It's reclaiming your power, allowing yourself to feel fully, and still knowing you're that bitch, even if your nose is red from crying, and you haven't gotten out of bed for three days. This is about demystifying the surface-level version of healing that dominates internet spaces for views and stepping into real transformation via grief, rage, shame, and guilt. You're going to fall apart. You know that's a part of the process. But you will rise hotter, wiser, and more powerful than ever.

Next up, I want to introduce you to one final tool for you to add to your trauma-transmuting tool kit. This one is literally written in the stars: it's your astrology chart.

CHAPTER 9

STOP BLAMING THE STARS AND READ THE DAMN CHART

Millionaires don't believe in astrology, billionaires do.
–J.P. MORGAN

I used to think astrology was complete bullshit.

While in medical school, I was deeply entrenched in left-brain logic and evidence-based everything. My world was dissected into clinical trials, diagnoses, and biochemical pathways. If it couldn't be peer reviewed, it didn't exist. As a student of science, I didn't understand why people would trust astrology. It didn't make sense that twelve zodiac signs could apply to billions of people across the world.

I think part of why I resisted it for so long was because of how I first encountered it. Growing up in India, astrology was everywhere. And a lot of it was...let's just say, deeply unscientific. I remember my grandmother once dragged me to this random-ass river in Punjab to toss some sort of metal object into the water. It was part of a Vedic ritual called *upai*, which basically means "solution." It describes the steps taken to solve a problem or overcome some challenge. For example, if you have a heavy Saturn in your chart, you're supposed to throw money at it. Literally. Give one lakh rupees to beggars. Every solution had some sort of ritual. Wear this gemstone on that finger. Donate this, wear that, chant this, face that direction. It was all superstition to me.

It didn't help that I was surrounded by people in residency who felt the same. I remember a particular moment so vividly it still makes me cringe. I was in residency and had this massive crush on a guy. What can I say, I had mommy issues and low self worth. Classic situationship vibes. We were midargument one day, and I tried to lighten the mood by joking, "God, this is such a Virgo thing to do."

Without missing a beat, he looked me dead in the eye and said, "I don't go out with girls who believe in horoscopes." Hysterical. Such a big synchronicity again. The Universe sending me another mirror and a slap in the face to step into my purpose.

It was rude and condescending. I was totally embarrassed, and the interaction reinforced my skepticism. But the Universe works in mysterious ways, and I truly think the interaction was divinely timed.

Even as I started exploring spirituality more, I avoided astrology. And yet, astrology kept finding me. Through friends, healing circles—everywhere I went, someone was bringing up charts and houses and retrogrades. People would casually ask,

"Do you know your moon sign? What's your rising?" And I'd respond with the only thing I knew: "I'm a Virgo. That's all I got."

It wasn't until I started working with my coach, Meera, that my perspective did a full 180. She had a background in esoteric astrology, and during our very first sessions, when I was totally lost after quitting residency, she asked me what my Midheaven is. We were talking about life purpose and specifically about what I wanted to do now that I had left residency. And I had no damn clue what came next. I told her my Midheaven was in Scorpio. She just smiled and said nothing. But in that smile, I could tell she could see something about my career in my chart. I didn't fully understand it yet, but I knew there was meaning there.

Because I'm a 1/3 profile in Human Design (shout out to my fellow HD nerds), I went full student mode. I started reading everything I could get my hands on and tracing the lineage of astrology through history. What I found blew my damn mind. Astrology wasn't this fluffy fortune cookie BS people made it out to be. It was an ancient practice soaked in symbolism and science. It was both mathematical and mystical at the same time. I learned that up until the 16th century, to go to medical school you needed to study both astrology and astronomy. And all the way up to the industrial revolution, it was considered a science. The more I learned, the more I fell into this thrilling love affair with astrology. And now it's hilarious to look back and see that I quit residency to become a psychological astrologer.

Also, what are the odds that my dog's name is Pluto? Synchronicity and magic once again. I had no idea when I named him nine and a half years ago that, fast forward a decade, I would be an astrologer. My 10th house (the house of career, legacy, reputation) has six Scorpio placements, with its traditional ruler being planet Mars and modern ruler, none other than Pluto!

Because astrology is an intricate and nuanced system, I can't teach you everything there is to know about astrology in one chapter. That's also not what this book is about. Personally, I am fascinated that when NASA discovers something new or when Neil Armstrong landed on the Moon, it's celebrated as the advancement of science and technology, but when astrologers use planets it's considered delulu. But, like I mentioned previously, this is a planet of free will. You get to choose your truth. Astrology is mine.

There are plenty of books available to help you deep dive into astrological studies like I did, and I share several of these resources in this chapter. This chapter's purpose is to teach you how to understand astrology as a trauma-informed, psychologically grounded tool to: uncover unconscious patterns, identify inherited wounds, develop deeper self-compassion, and make empowered, conscious choices. Let's dive in.

FATE VERSES FREEWILL

Before we get any further in this chapter, I want to clear up one giant misconception around astrology: Astrology *can* be a predictive tool but you still have free will.

At least it shouldn't be used for the *sole* purpose of predicting your future. And you shouldn't rely solely on your chart when it comes to making big life decisions. Can it help with those things and give you guidance? Sure. But it's so important to remember to never give your power away to anyone or anything else, including an astrology chart or the person reading it. Always use discernment. You *always* have free will, and it's up to you to hold personal accountability when making choices.

An astrologer should never hold the power to decide what your soul came here to choose.

Just because a chart shows potential doesn't mean it shows what will actually happen. It shows possibility, not prediction. Your lived reality depends on your choices, your boundaries, your healing, and your willingness to take action. A chart can reflect the energy or pattern you're working with, but it won't tell you what decision to make or how your story ends. That part is on you.

And trust me, I get the temptation. My twin flame and I have almost identical placements. It's mind blowing. On paper, we look like the perfect pair, but that definitely has not been the case. That just means our charts mirror each other in ways that reveal shared wounds and shared potential.

WHAT ASTROLOGY *IS* HERE TO DO

Astrology requires a deep understanding of your individual chart and its unique energies. It is your soul's natal blueprint. While daily horoscopes are fun to read, they don't actually reflect full truth. You can't cram seven billion people into twelve categories and expect it to be anything other than entertainment.

I use astrology as a practical tool to maximize the potential of my client's chart. I use it to understand "the self." To me, astrology is a map of the psyche. It's a language that speaks to both the psychological and the spiritual layers of who we are—our patterns and our potential. When interpreted with depth, a chart can shine a light on the unconscious dynamics running your life. It can reveal ancestral influences (especially Chiron, south node, IC points in the chart) you didn't even know you were carrying, and it can help you make sense of the traumas that live in your body but don't belong to your personal timeline. It can guide you toward deeper healing, self-trust, and wholeness.

When you look at the full chart, it's not about putting people in boxes. It's not as one dimensional as simply knowing your sun sign. It's about uncovering the threads that connect your inner world to something much bigger than you.

When I took my first psychological astrology course, we didn't even talk about the sun sign until much later. It was, quite literally, the sixth thing we were taught to look at. It's your rising sign—the sign on the horizon at the exact moment of your birth—that individualizes your chart. Your rising sign sets the framework for your soul's assignment in this lifetime. Your life task. It's what defines your 12 houses. And it's determined by a narrow two-hour window, which means even someone born on the same day as you could have an entirely different life blueprint.

I personally use whole house systems for readings because it is ancient, Hellenistic astrology from the year 2 BC. The oldest house system. Please see which style resonates with your soul the most. Neither is wrong.

This is why surface-level astrology fails so many people. They read a generic horoscope based on just their sun sign, roll their eyes, and assume the whole system is fluff. But they're engaging with a version of astrology stripped of its complexity.

To use astrology in a meaningful way, you need to understand your entire chart: the planets, the aspects, the houses, the elements, the archetypes. You need to see how the energies intersect, challenge, and support one another. It's not "You're a Leo so you're confident." It's: "Your Leo sun is squaring your Scorpio moon in the 4th house while Saturn is sitting in your 2nd house of worth and income, so let's talk about how your early emotional environment is affecting your career right now." And don't even get me started on the precision of adding degrees. It feels like an intellectual orgasm to my Aquarius moon and Virgo sun.

See the difference?

This is why I always recommend getting your full chart read by a trained astrologer, someone who understands both the psychological and symbolic language of astrology.

ASTROLOGY THROUGH A JUNGIAN LENS

As a trained psychiatrist, I'd be remiss if I didn't mention psychological astrology, which was fathered by Carl Jung. His version of psychological astrology resonates with me because it treats the chart as more than a personality profile, seeing it as a symbolic map of the unconscious. It's less about categorizing traits and more about uncovering patterns, projections, and archetypal dynamics.

So, let's talk about Carl Jung, the black sheep of early psychiatry and the original bridge between science and soul. If Sigmund Freud was the father of psychoanalysis, Jung was the rebellious son who refused to cut the soul out of psychology.

They started out aligned, both men trying to legitimize the human psyche as something worth studying. But Freud, who came from a neurological background, was obsessed with keeping psychology "respectable" in the medical field. Everything had to be rational, observable, and explainable. Meanwhile, Jung was sitting in therapy sessions with patients who were having religious visions, archetypal dreams, and psychic breakthroughs, and he wasn't about to write that off as nonsense. He believed those experiences meant something.

That's where astrology came in.

Jung didn't use astrology for prediction. He used it as an archetypal map of the psyche. He believed that the birth chart could illuminate unconscious patterns, inner conflicts, and soul-level archetypes that shape our experience of reality. In other words, it could help us understand where we're stuck, why we keep repeating certain relational dynamics, and what we're here to grow through.

This was all part of what Jung called individuation: the lifelong process of becoming your most whole, integrated self. It's about becoming the version of you that is rooted in both your shadow and your light. The version of you that's guided by something deeper than ego: your true Self. Astrology, when used well, is one of the best tools I've ever found for supporting that process.

Individuation requires you to integrate the parts of yourself you've rejected, a process called shadow work; confront the inner masculine and feminine energies you've neglected, which Jung referred to as the anima and animus; and start listening to the unconscious wisdom that emerges in your dreams, synchronicities, and symbolic patterns. Astrology gives language to all of that.

When you use astrology as a tool for the psyche as well as the spirit, you see more than planetary placements in your chart; you're also looking at archetypes. You're seeing your unconscious mirrored back in symbolic form.

If you'd like to learn more about psychological astrology, I'd highly recommend reading *Jung on Astrology* by the man, the myth, the legend himself, C.G. Jung. I also highly recommend checking out the teachings and books by Liz Greene who was literally given a suitcase full of Jung's notes by his daughter, who was a professional astrologer. Yes, you heard me correctly *Jung's daughter* was a professional astrologer.

WHAT A CHART *REALLY* TELLS YOU

If you've ever looked at a full natal chart and felt overwhelmed, you're not alone. It's a lot. Most people think astrology stops at your sun sign, but the sun is one small piece of the picture. It's your outer ego. The leading character or superhero suit you put on. It's a costume. A trained astrologer will usually look at your

If the first step in alchemy is collapse (hello darkness), then the second is cleansing. One way to do that is by feeling our feelings. Let it all out, my friend.

In classical alchemy, this is the Albedo phase. This is where self-awareness comes out and the chaos starts to clear. The grief begins to move. But here's the catch: Feeling your feelings is terrifying. If you're not used to it, you're going to be *hella* uncomfortable, especially if you grew up in a home where emotions were punished or pathologized. The hard reality is most people don't know what it's like to actually sit with their emotions.

Why is feeling your feelings so uncomfortable? There are layers to that answer. The first reason is trauma, plain and simple. According to Family Constellations, trauma fragments the soul. When you experience trauma, whether it was in utero in your mom's belly, in your childhood, or a burden that belongs to your ancestors, your soul escapes your body. Because of that, you now live with your head up. Trauma makes you feel unsafe in your body, and the nervous system copes by dissociating. And you're not going to feel what's going on in the body if your mind is doing everything it can to stay out of it.

I used to shame myself for dissociating, telling myself that I was defective for not being able to stay in my body. But dissociation is never defective. Biologically, it's brilliant. It was my nervous system trying to keep me alive. Escaping into my mind because it wasn't safe to be in my body.

The second reason has to do with the collective shadow. We live in a world that worships logic, where emotional intelligence is rising sign first, because your rising sign shapes your house placements, which in turn influence how planetary energies actually show up in your life. Every addition further on is seen through the lens of, "Does this help the rising sign or does it hinder or challenge it?" Your midheaven or the Medium Coeli (MC), often called the career or vocation, is the person you are supposed to become toward the end of your life by fulfilling your life task, which is marked by your rising or ascendant sign.

But even then, a chart doesn't tell you who you are; it tells you what energies you're working with. It shows you patterns, wounds, potential, and so much more, but it doesn't tell you how your life will turn out. That part can be a transformational tool.

Let me give you an example.

I have Saturn in Pisces in the second house, and it's retrograde. The second house rules things like income, resources, and self-worth. Saturn is the taskmaster, the great father. It's the planet of time, structure, karma, and lessons learned the hard way. When it's retrograde, the energy turns inward. So what does that mean for me?

It means I've carried a brutal inner critic. This is the voice that doesn't let me celebrate a win for more than five seconds before whispering, "You should've done more." When I first read about that placement, I cried because it was the first time I felt validated in that part of myself. It gave me language to describe something I'd always felt. And now that I have that language, I can start to reframe my thoughts. When that inner critic shows up, I can tell her to shut the hell up because I know it's my Saturn in Pisces showing up to stir the pot. It's here to teach me long-lasting self worth and that only comes with time and mastery.

That's the gift of astrology when it's used responsibly. Once you can name the pattern, you can work with it. You can transmute it and stop projecting it onto everyone else and start actually healing it.

USING ASTROLOGY TO IDENTIFY INHERITED WOUNDS

One of the most powerful ways I use astrology in my work is to identify ancestral patterns—the unconscious loops we inherit from our family line that live in our nervous system, our behavior, and our sense of identity. These are the wounds we didn't choose but still have to reckon with.

Jung called this the collective unconscious, the idea that we're not born into a blank slate but into an energetic field of inherited archetypes and unfinished business. These archetypes are transpersonal patterns, things like the martyr, the addict, the absent father, the wounded healer. They live in myths, religions, and family systems. And until they're made conscious, we act them out.

Your chart can show you which of these patterns you're carrying, whether you realize it or not.

For example, maybe you have Saturn in the first house, which can reflect heavy burden on your shoulders or early parentification. Maybe your Mars sits in the same house as your father's natal Mars, and you've inherited not just his drive but his volatility. Maybe Pluto's sitting in your eighth house, lighting up ancestral trauma like a flare.

When people come to me with patterns they can't break like relationship sabotage, self-worth issues, burnout, overgiving, astrology helps us see what isn't theirs to carry. Sometimes what we call "personality" is actually family loyalty in disguise.

I think Systemic and Family Constellations mixed with astrology could be the future. What do you think?

YOUR CHART IS NOT YOUR FINAL FATE

I need to be clear about this: Your chart is not your final fate. Yes I do believe in destiny; however, knowledge is power.

Your birth chart doesn't cause anything. It reflects what's already present. It shows the energetic blueprint you're working with in this lifetime. That includes your strengths, your wounds, your potential, your inner conflicts, what you look for in ideal partners.

Take transits, for example: Saturn returns, Uranus transits— these are timing tools. Saturn causes delays and Uranus speeds up time.They tend to activate growth, bring tension to the surface, or highlight parts of your life that are ready to evolve. But they don't force anything. They don't make your relationship fall apart. They don't *cause* a career change. What they do is mirror where you are in your own process. They show you what energy is available and what you might want to pay attention to.

PRACTICAL ASTROLOGY

When I first started learning astrology, the doctor and science student part of me wanted to change the narrative around it being dismissed as pseudoscience. One of my passions, out of the million I have, is making astrology practical for the client. Because honestly, it doesn't matter if your Neptune is retrograde at 18 degrees in Capricorn because WTF does that even mean for a real person's actual life?

What I came to realize is that when astrology is misunderstood, it can easily feed fear. But when it's used well, it becomes a tool for discernment and for aligning with the natural flow of life.

Here are a list of the few most practical ways I use astrology:

1. **Astrocartography:** This branch of astrology maps how the positions of the planets at the time of your birth influence different locations on Earth. For example, a Moon rising line might bring happiness and joy, while a Venus line can bring experiences of love and beauty. In short, it's like geography meets astrology, uniquely designed for your natal chart. Shout-out to Helena Woods, an amazing astrocartographer who helped me relocate from the East Coast to California!

2. **Zodiacal Releasing:** Think of this as astrology on steroids. It's a timing technique from Hellenistic astrology, popularized by astrologer Chris Brennan. It's a time-lord system that divides your life into chapters and subchapters, showing when different themes such as career or health are most active. It's super cool. And Chris Brennan, in my eyes, is the GOAT of astrology teachers.

Feel free to look him up on YouTube if you're curious and want to dive into more of this esoteric stuff.

3. **Electional Astrology:** This branch focuses on choosing the most favorable time to begin an important action like launching a business, hosting an event, or releasing a product, for the best possible outcome.

4. **Psychological Astrology:** This is *my* niche as a former half-psychiatrist. (Fun fact: Carl Jung and I are both Aquarius risings with Scorpio Midheavens.) This approach helps you see where your deepest wounds, challenges, gifts, strengths, and fortunes lie so you can maximize your soul's unique potential.

Ultimately, astrology is a mirror for your relationship with free will. It can illuminate what's unconscious. It can help you understand your patterns. It can point you toward integration. But it will never do the work for you. That part is always yours.

HOW TO USE ASTROLOGY IN A TRAUMA-INFORMED WAY

Astrology can be a powerful tool for healing, but only if it's used with care. When you're doing deep psychological or ancestral work, or when you're in a vulnerable state, it can help find guidance and clarity on next steps and challenging transits.

A good astrologer will reflect your chart back to you in a way that feels clear, compassionate, and aligned. They won't make dramatic claims, and they won't try to scare you into action. I look for practitioners who are trauma-informed, people who understand nervous system regulation, consent, and the weight of what it means to speak into someone's psyche. When you're already in a vulnerable state, flooding yourself with random, unfiltered astrology content online can actually create more confusion and dysregulation.

Be cautious about astrology you find on social media. There's a difference between educational content and what I call "street astrology," which is overgeneralized hot takes about signs, relationships, or planetary transits that leave you more confused than supported. If it sounds extreme, clickbaity, or too good to be true, it probably is.

When you're ready to explore your chart, start with someone who has both training and integrity. Let your intuition lead. If you're someone who enjoys apps, I recommend The Pattern app. It's an accessible way to start exploring the themes in your chart without getting overwhelmed by all the technical language, and it's freaking accurate.

NOW YOU KNOW

You don't need to become an astrologer to benefit from astrology. There are plenty of trained astrologers out there for those seeking help and guidance. Find someone who's in alignment for your individual path and healing journey.

Just knowing the basics of your chart—your rising sign, your Moon, your Saturn, your Chiron—can start to give shape to things you've always felt but could never explain. It gives you language for your inner world. It helps you see what's yours, what was passed down, and what you're here to alchemize.

That alone can be life-changing. Awareness is always the first step to change.

Astrology isn't about using the chart to label yourself, it's about using it to witness yourself with more compassion, more precision, and more power. You stop saying "I'm just like this," and start saying, "This is the energy I'm working with, and now I know how to work with it."

The more conscious you become, the more you begin the true work of this book: the journey of individuation. In the next chapter, we'll talk about what it really means to become whole.

Part 3

REBIRTH

CHAPTER 10

INDIVIDUATION IS A BLOOD SPORT

Knowing your own darkness is the best medicine for dealing with the darkness of others.
–CARL JUNG

Yes, my great-grandmother killed her husband.

You've already heard this story. I'm bringing it up again now because that story planted the first shadow I've been trying to heal my entire life.

When I first learned about it, I didn't have the language or tools to process it, so I locked it in a box and buried it inside the cage of shadows in my subconscious. But it never stopped humming beneath the surface. When I started my healing journey and opened up Pandora's box, that fun fact about my family history shot out along with all the other shame, fear, and regrets I'd buried inside.

My great-grandmother's story is a big reason behind why I wrote this book.

It would be easy to reduce her to a headline: a woman gone mad, consumed by rage, doing the unthinkable. But that's not how I see her anymore. I see her as a woman who was trying to free herself. A woman trapped in golden handcuffs. Shackles disguised as privilege.

I'm not trying to justify anybody's actions. Yes she did what she did, and she was held responsible; she served time. Personally, I think she was kind of a baddie. I remember listening to Chris Brennan's astrology podcast on the archetype of Scorpio, and in his classic straight-faced dark humor, he said, "It's not Scorpio unless someone dies."

But when I think about my great-grandmother's story, I see it through the lens of privilege. My family comes from blue blood, and I'm the first working woman in my lineage for generations. From the outside looking in, the women in my family seemed to have it pretty damn good. Which makes me wonder: *Was she actually living in freedom, or was she trapped by golden handcuffs?*

Golden handcuffs are the privileges, comforts, and social advantages that look enviable from the outside but make you feel like a captive on the inside. Sometimes they're a package deal with violence, control, or manipulation hidden behind luxury. Essentially, when you're strapped in golden handcuffs, you're trapped in a golden cage.

These golden handcuffs can manifest as societal or familial pressures that dictate how you should live or behave, often leading to feelings of obligation or guilt, which comes with receiving money or gifts. It can be hard to be genuinely grateful when deep inside you fear a sense of unspoken control. Even when these restraints come from a place of love or care, such as expectations from family members who want the best for you, they can still limit your ability to pursue your true desires and identity.

So, I have to wonder about my great-grandmother. Did she feel like she was wearing golden handcuffs?

If she did, she didn't have the tools or the language to process her pain and break free the way I have. She didn't have access to this kind of work. But I do. And so do you. Thanks to our ancestors.

Every generation refines what the last one couldn't. As we heal the emotional stories we've inherited, we also have to look at how these stories affect the external parts of our lives. Especially in our relationship with money.

MONEY EQUALS LOVE IN THE FIELD

When we talk about freedom, we can't ignore the energetic threads that tie love, survival, and money together. Our ancestors didn't just pass down emotional patterns to us, they passed down the way they experienced both love and material security. In the quantum field, money and love run on the same current. Both are energies of giving and receiving. When love flows freely in a family system, money tends to flow too. When love is blocked, whether that is through guilt, shame, exclusion, control, or unprocessed trauma, money often mirrors that stuckness.

To understand our patterns with money, we have to look at where they began: in the way we first learned to give and receive love. Love is so important for the evolution of a child. In childhood, love is the energy and force which nurtures, protects, and helps a child grow. When you become an adult and face the real world this energy of love—that energy that fed, clothed, and protected you as a child—is replaced with the energy of money. It's *money* that helps you put food on the table, provide shelter, and nurture yourself and fulfil your material desires.

The way love was given (or not given) and was perceived by a child, will shape the way an adult relates to money in terms of attachment style. In other words, our earliest experiences of love become the blueprint for how we experience safety, worth, and flow with money.

To explain further with an example, let's say that when you were growing up that love felt conditional for a plethora of various reasons. This conditional love could have made you feel anxiously attached to money: causing you to think it may be taken away or should be hoarded. Or, when thinking about love, let's say love felt unsafe or dangerous to you due to various forms of abuse. This could make you lean more avoidant when it comes to your attachment style to money.

Luckily, beyond all the root cause healing work that Constellations Therapy offers, it also helps with money work. Constellations is an excellent manifestation tool. I don't mean manifestation in the "wish-it-and-get-it" sense, but Family Constellations can help you manifest your desires by clearing the ancestral and energetic blocks that keep abundance from flowing naturally. You can use it to determine rates for your services, call in aligned clients, and overall to draw more material abundance into your life.

The quantum field is very pro humans being materialistic because any avoidance of earthly desires is seen as a form of spiritual bypassing. The highest spiritual experience of a soul being incarnated on our planet earth is actually the material, meaning the ability to bring consciousness, love, and integrity into our human, physical lives. After all, what is the point of all this healing if it's not practically useful?

The relationship your ancestors carried with money is also passed down epigenetically and environmentally to progeny. When you help heal your money wounds, you help heal your lineage's relationship with money. My intention is to introduce this awareness so we can all live more balanced spiritual and material lives.

So as we near the end of this book, the first of my final invitations is to notice how money shows up in your life. What expectations, fears, or inherited beliefs are keeping you bound? Who told you it had to be that way? And then ask yourself what it would look like to:

- Take one action that allows you to step out of that pattern
- Say no to what you were taught you're supposed to want
- Make a financial decision that prioritizes alignment over approval
- Trust in the unknown over fear

Individuation is the conscious choice to become who your soul came here to be, not who your lineage, trauma, or culture told you to be. That choice is the most sacred act of healing you can make, and that's what this final chapter is about. This is the purpose of evolution. The final takeaway of Family Constellations is that Life must take precedence over trauma. Our purpose of being alive at this time is to live a full life in honor of your ancestors, return their fate, and channel their gifts with honor and reverence.

FROM SHADOW TO SELF

We've been through a lot together in these pages: shame, rage, dissociation, grief, ancestral trauma, addiction, nervous system repair, and the raw truth of what it means to face your pain and transmute it instead of running from it.

- We've tackled the myth that healing is about erasing trauma and have seen that trauma isn't a flaw to eliminate but a doorway to deeper invitation to self-understanding.

- We've learned how shame—especially inherited and collective shame—keeps us stuck in patterns of fear and have learned how to face the shame cage with courage and to witness our story without judgement.

- We've covered how trauma lives in the body, not the mind and have seen why safety is so important before healing and have learned that spiritual practices can't override a dysregulated nervous system.

- We've explored the nature of victimhood, how it makes us choose familiar hell over unfamiliar heaven.

- We've learned how to hold compassion for shame and now know it's just trying to keep us small and safe.

- We have illuminated the importance of free will in rewriting inherited patterns.

- We've walked through the nonlinear messy steps of healing: curiosity, avoidance, feeling, integration, and choice.

- We've seen how the balance of masculine and feminine energy are sacred polarities we all carry as we've reframed protection, love, and intuition as interconnected, fluid forces within the healing journey. It is truly this inner union that reflects in our reality outside.

- We've reclaimed grief, depression, and breakdowns as vital parts of transformation, not signs of failure. We've learned how to move through the blackest parts of healing with style, sovereignty, and a refusal to self-abandon. We can be depressed, anxious, crazy, and still be sexy AF. #depresexy

- And we've covered how astrology is in fact the oldest fucking science. It is an excellent tool for soul-level self-awareness and practical growth as we've learned how to work with our birth charts to uncover karmic patterns and portals of planetary energy to work with.

And now we're about to move on to the final phase of alchemy: where everything that's been burned down and purified begins to integrate. Where the gold is transmuted from the darkness. This chapter is the final integration. This is where you embody what you've learned and (try) to become the medicine.

In Jungian psychology, the act of becoming your whole, authentic, and sovereign Self—separate from ego, family, culture, or shadow projection—is called *individuation*. It's a lifelong journey, but it has key moments of breakthrough where the inner self integrates. This can be one of those moments for you, *if* you are game.

INDIVIDUATION IS A BLOOD SPORT (NOT A SPA TREATMENT)

You don't reclaim your soul without shedding a few identities first.

Here's the second invitation: Look at the roles you've been performing as good daughter, strong one, peacemaker, rebel. Ask yourself which ones are rooted in your soul, and which ones were wired in through survival.

Individuation is the process of becoming who your soul came here to be. It's the lifelong work of integrating all the parts you've disowned: your shadow, your rage, your grief, your brilliance, your feminine and masculine energies, and everything in between. I wish my self-created perfectionism had no business in the land of individuation. It's a messy and honest place to be, and it usually involves a few ego deaths and some loud sobbing to get there.

Carl Jung described individuation as the process of integrating the unconscious into the conscious mind. That means merging your ego with the Self, the deepest and most authentic part of your psyche.

According to Jung, these are the key features of individuation:

1. Integration of the Shadow

This involves confronting and integrating the disowned, suppressed, or rejected parts of yourself (aka the things you might often project onto others).

In this stage, you make a choice. You stop pretending to be the "good one," the "strong one," or the "enlightened one," and start dragging your disowned parts into the light. Rage, envy, control, shame; it's all you, babe.

If loud, confident, sexual, or emotionally expressive people piss you off or make you uncomfortable, it's probably because you were taught that you weren't allowed to be that way. So you pushed those parts of yourself underground—maybe as a kid, maybe as a teenager—and now when they show up in other people, they trigger the hell out of you. That's called projection.

2. Reclaiming Your Inner Masculine and Feminine (Anima/ Animus)

Jung believed that within every man is a feminine aspect (anima), and within every woman is a masculine aspect (animus). Recognizing and integrating these energies brings inner balance.

So if you're a woman who's terrified of being assertive (like me who often feels like I'm too intense for a woman) or a man who's been taught to shut down his emotions, that's exactly where your growth lives. This is your soft gentle nudge.

Individuation asks you to stop performing gender and start reclaiming the full spectrum of who you are, the structure and the fluidity, the clarity and the chaos. You need both. We all do.

3. Ego vs Self: Who's Really Driving?

Your ego is the part of you that manages your image, avoids rejection, and keeps you alive. Your Self is the deeper, wiser intelligence, intuition within you, or the part that doesn't need to prove shit.

Individuation asks you to stop letting the ego run the show and start listening to the Self. So that your ego can be in service to your soul and not visa versa. A healthy ego is important.

4. Dreams, Symbols, and WTF Moments

Your unconscious doesn't use words. It speaks in symbols, synchronicities, myths, dreams, basically the weird stuff you want to write off as coincidence. Don't write it off.

If you keep dreaming of wolves, if you keep seeing the same number, if you feel like the Universe is sending you messages, I'm telling you it is.

Dreams, synchronicities, and myths are messengers during the individuation process, guiding you toward hidden truths and integration.

5. Wholeness > Perfection

This process isn't about becoming a better person. It's about becoming *your* person. Your wholeness will not look like anyone else's.

I'm gonna be really honest; this is still my biggest challenge. My Chiron is in Virgo, the wound of perfectionism. Work in progress, baby. As we near the end of this book, I feel that part of me rise up, trying to criticize: *Who do you think you are, teaching people self-compassion when you struggle with it so much yourself?*

The truth is, I'm not perfect. I'm real. And for that, I'm proud. So please don't idolize me. I'm still integrating these lessons myself. I'm a forever seeker, a student of this life. I haven't even been on this journey that long; I'm just stepping into my 30s.

So come walk this path with me. We're here to integrate, to embrace the full spectrum of our humanity, and to stop trying to amputate the parts of ourselves we were taught to hide.

Let's recap: Individuation is about becoming who you truly are, beyond society's expectations, your childhood conditioning, or the mask (persona) you wear. It's the sacred, alchemical process of turning your fragmented self into a unified Self.

YOU DON'T NEED A GURU

If you've made it this far, I want to say something that might surprise you:

Take the credit.

If something shifted in you while reading this book—if it stirred something buried, touched a nerve, lit a fire, or made you see yourself in these pages—it's not because I'm a genius. (I mean, I *am*, but you know what I mean.) Every reader's win is my win. This is a huge part of my life's purpose: to help heal shame on this planet. So people stop living dual lives. So lineages can break free from secrets, those hidden cages we're taught to carry.

You picked this book up at the exact right moment. You were ready. *You* read it. *You* faced it. *You* did the work. Every time I thank Meera for her healing help, she always reflects it back to me: *I did this. I did the work. I wrote this book.* And honestly, words of affirmation are definitely my love language; as a Virgo who struggles with self-critical tendencies, I need them.

But here's the truth: I'm still right here next to you. I'm still shedding layers. I'm still fucking up and learning from my mistakes (hello, Human Design Generator + investigative martyr 1/3 profile). I'm still observing my patterns and figuring out how to let them go. And while writing this book, I went through the whole process all over again. I fell into a dark night of the soul and had to walk straight through it to integration. It sucked. But I came out the other side closer to my true self.

And I know it won't be the last time. It'll happen again and again. Because this—this messy, gritty, beautiful path—is a lifelong process. Damn those Scorpio placements.

So if you're looking for a guru, keep walking. You don't need another voice telling you what to do. You need to listen to the one inside you. Heal your relationship with your parents. Heal for your ancestors. Listen to the voice that's been whispering underneath the conditioning and the shame. Learn to tolerate the guilt and embrace the person you know deep down you were always meant to be.

And if all this book did was help you remember that? That's enough.

Here's the final invitation: Take what landed. Leave what didn't. Burn this book if you want. I won't take it personally.

But if you remember anything, let it be this:

You came to this planet to live as your *whole self*. Not the masked version. Not the obedient version. You are the answer to your ancestors' prayers. You are the true one. The free one. The one who gets to choose what your life looks like all while still belonging to your family tree.

So use discernment and choose.

There is no going back now.

ACKNOWLEDGEMENTS

I would like to start this section by thanking my ancestors for all of their hard work, sacrifices, and love. I pray that I always continue to possess the humility to remember where I came from.

I am so grateful to my maternal lineage for the boldness they passed on to me. It is an honor to unlock the wisdom of the dark feminine. I equally want to express gratitude to my paternal lineage, including being able to channel for astrological natal chart readings, which is a beautiful ancestral gift that I now get to share with the world as my vocation. I am so proud to be Punjabi and to belong to this lineage of true heart-led warriors in this lifetime.

Most importantly, I would like to thank my wonderful set of parents, my father and my mother, for this beautiful gift of life. My mother is a true visionary Goddess who chose my name before I was born and came all the way to the United States to give me the ultimate gift of freedom by birthing me in this country. It is an absolute privilege to finish this book in my birth land, Los Angeles. No amount of words will ever describe our soul-level love and bond, Mother. Thank you for passing on psychic gifts, which activated early in life, all thanks to you. I am just like you, Mumma; I am a writer too. I will always belong to you even as I continue to individuate and follow my own path and calling.

Next: My father, thank you for loving me unconditionally, Papa, even though I chose a different vocation from what you intended for me. I am just like you, Papa, I will serve the world in my own unique ways like you saved so many lives during COVID. It is an honor to be your daughter. Thank you for the gifts of wisdom, bravery, and integrity. I still remember when I was a little girl struggling with academics and self-doubt, when you wrote on my register "IM-possible", and said "Look Meher, even the word "impossible says 'I'm possible." This is why I never gave up on my dreams. Thank you for everything.

My next heartfelt gratitude is to my teacher and mentor: Meera Mohan. You helped me transform my life, you held space for all my shame that I was so good at hiding, my unacknowledged pain and emotions. Thank you for showing me that the world in fact can be trusted once again. Thank you for reconnecting me to my life purpose, my intuition, and body. There is so much I have learned from you, that real inner confidence is quiet, that we all can be alchemists, and reclaim our magic. Thank you for helping me grow up from a child to an adult in the kindest, softest, and loving manner. It's the grand trine. Most of all, no matter how much I grow, achieve, and expand to always have humility.

Moving on to Mia: The baddest witch out there. Thank you for being a true leader for the feminine in this world. Thank you for helping heal rage in women and for all that you do for our wonderful Mother Earth. What a beautiful life purpose! I always struggled with thinking I am too intense and powerful for a woman, until I had the honor to meet you. Sending you much love and respect.

Last but not the least, and this is the one I struggle with the most: Thank you to *myself*. Meher, you are one brave and powerful woman. Thank you for putting in the work, thank you for your courage to quit a career at 29 to start from scratch again. Thank you for writing this book and speaking your truth no matter how scared you were to express your authenticity and intensity. My Shadows, you were bloody and painful, but you were the medicine I didn't realise I needed. So thank you, Shadow. You weren't evil. You were the hidden potential. I finally found my shadow gold. So thank you, Meher, for being so brave, bold, vulnerable, intelligent, driven, and, of course, hilarious and sexy.

My purpose is to show the world that not all wealthy people are evil, and that with great power *does* come great responsibility. That power in the right hands can transform the collective and help heal so much pain.

And to my dearest reader: Thank you for taking the time to read my book and/or listening to the audio version. Thank you for the trust. May love flow through your lineage and life unconditionally.

THE MEDICINE IN FAMILY CONSTELLATIONS

This work doesn't end at the close of this book.

If this book awoke something deep within you and you are feeling that call to go deeper—I dare you to do it. I believe in your bravery.

I invite you to explore Family Constellations.

Family Constellations changed my life. It gave shape to the shadows I couldn't name or honestly didn't even know existed in my family system. It showed me what belonged to me and what never did. It gave me a way to move beyond just understanding my trauma to actually transmuting it and honoring it without letting it drag me down.

The truth is, you can do all the journaling, therapy, and nervous system work in the world, but if you're still stuck in a pattern that won't move, it might not have started with you.

Family Constellations helps you uncover and release the unconscious loyalties, inherited beliefs, and generational trauma that are keeping you stuck. It's not about blaming those who came before you. It's about reordering the family system so your soul can breathe again and love can finally flow through.

My intention for this book is that you remember that you do have the power to choose who you become—no matter what you've inherited. Yes, as an astrologer, I do believe in destiny and fate, but I also believe in cocreating your destiny with the Universe. Like my father would often say to me, "Meher, success is half hard work and half takdeer (that means "fate" in Hindi). For me, Family Constellations helped me get there. I want to share this secret with the world, which potentially could do the same for you.

If you'd like to learn more, please visit my website at www. drmeherchahal.com.

And to you, dear reader: May your own ancestors' shadows guide you home to yourself, so you never have to live a dual life again. My wish is for you to have more joy, love, and abundance in your life but above all the courage to be disliked and still authentically be yourself.

With gratitude,
Dr. Chahal

ABOUT THE AUTHOR

Dr. Meher Chahal is an Indian-American doctor, psychological astrologer, Jungian coach, and visionary entrepreneur trained in Family Constellation therapy. Born into a lineage marked by her mother's schizophrenia and a murder in her maternal line, she experienced firsthand the weight of trauma that Western medicine alone could not explain. After a decade in medicine and psychiatry, she left the conventional path to follow a deeper calling. Her discovery and training in Family Constellations revealed a system she calls the most powerful healing modality on the planet—one that unites the science of epigenetics with the wisdom of the soul. Passionate about bridging the gap between Eastern spiritual healing and logical Western medicine, she guides others through *Unlicensed Medicine* in freeing ourselves of the shadows of our past and ancestors, and illuminating the delicate balance between belonging to our family systems and personal individuation for evolution. Making this therapy practically useful, she reveals how money, love, sexuality, and power are deeply connected in the Family Constellations quantum field. She lives in California with her two Maltese pups—and has a love of dark humor, which is her favorite survival skill.

www.ingramcontent.com/pod-product-compliance
Lightning Source LLC
Chambersburg PA
CBHW071728120626
46550CB00002B/439